Silent Sacrifice on the Homefront

Military spouses share their quests to fit career with marriage, motherhood, and military life

Michelle Still Mehta

Silent sacrifice on the homefront: Military spouses share their quests to fit career with marriage, motherhood, and military life

ISBN 9781729213704

To James, who has shared his military journey with me, and given us an adventure of a lifetime. I wouldn't change a single minute.

Table of Contents

Author's Note   1

Chapter 1 – Introduction   5

Chapter 2 – Marriage   17

Chapter 3 – Motherhood   75

Chapter 4 – Military Life   117

Chapter 5 – Integrating the 3 Ms   155

Chapter 6 – A Call to Action   191

References   203

Acknowledgments   207

Author's Note

When I decided to go back to graduate school to pursue a doctorate in human and organizational systems, it was purely for selfish reasons. I thought this would be the key to maintaining my career as a military spouse, bolstering the credentials I needed to build and sustain an independent consulting business to take with me at every assignment. As it turns out, my graduate work led to a new calling to support other military spouses grappling with their own career challenges.

Like all new graduate students, one of my first tasks was to pick a topic for my dissertation. I was particularly interested in researching issues related to the psychology of working life, and how work shapes one's identity and sense of self. I had personally experienced two very different ends of the professional spectrum – extreme overwork at a consulting firm that gave me a sense of achievement but wore me down mentally and physically, and involuntary unemployment as a military spouse overseas that left me searching for self-worth and purpose. I thought I would research some aspect of how work factors into our psyches, but had no inkling at the time that I would connect any of this to military life. Even after 7 years of marriage, I was still uncomfortable with my military spouse identity and preferred to think of the Air Force as simply "my husband's job." I admired my husband's desire to serve his country, but I did not want his service to determine how I defined myself.

This all changed one weekend when I attended a seminar on systems theory in Bethel, Maine. Hosted by Charlie and Edie Seashore, legendary thought leaders in organization development, this seminar had a reputation for changing people's lives. I was told that after attending this seminar, I would never see things quite the same way again. And that was true. When it was my turn to present an analysis of my own system, my life, and my work, I was shocked when the other students and professors in my group almost unanimously reflected back to me that I had an opportunity to

1

make a difference in the military system. Why didn't I explore how other military spouses have dealt with the same career and identity challenges I had been struggling with? Suddenly, I had a dissertation topic I had never considered before: How does military life affect a career-oriented military spouse's sense of self (Mehta, 2012)? That is the question I set out to answer, and this book is a compilation of the stories I gathered during the course of my research.

Throughout the 4½ years I spent in graduate school, I, too, was living the life of a military spouse. I applied to graduate school when we lived in Las Vegas and our oldest daughter was a 1-year-old. I began my studies when we moved to Washington, DC, for a Pentagon assignment, and was ready to begin my dissertation research when two wonderfully disruptive events occurred: Our son was born and we received orders to go to Ramstein Air Base, Germany. So I put my research plans on hold, took a 6-month leave from school, and packed up our family to move overseas. After getting settled in Germany, I took up my research again and began to interview Air Force wives stationed at Ramstein.

I chose a sample for my study that made sense for my research question and methodology, but was not meant to represent the entire military spouse population. I decided to interview a group of spouses that were homogeneous in several ways so that I could more easily draw conclusions from a relatively small sample of individuals. Everyone in my study was a female Air Force spouse stationed at Ramstein, who had experienced a Permanent Change of Station (PCS) move at least once for every 3 years of marriage, and had expressed a desire to be employed. Among this population, I intentionally selected a diverse pool of participants based on rank of service member and the spouse's self-reported ethnic identity. These women ranged from young newlyweds on their first assignment to seasoned spouses going on three decades of military life.

All research participants were volunteers whom I solicited through spouse clubs, local message boards, and my personal spouse network. For the final interview group, I did not select any spouses I personally socialized with or who were in my husband's chain of command. I conducted this research during the spring of 2011.

In total, I interviewed 21 Air Force spouses, all of whom are included in this book. The interviews were recorded and transcribed, and the questions focused on their experiences and feelings related to their employment. I began each interview by asking the individual to share her timeline of each of her military assignments. We discussed her employment, or lack thereof, at each assignment, and explored how she felt about her situation and herself along the way. Each participant agreed to have her story told anonymously in published form, and all names in this book and in my dissertation are fictitious.

After I completed my interviews and conducted a thorough content analysis of the data, I began to look for patterns and themes. The most consistent and striking theme is that of the "3 Ms," which is the basis for this book. That is, the spouses who seem happiest with themselves and their careers are those who mindfully fit their employment into three key areas of their lives: Marriage, Motherhood, and Military Life. Those who struggle are those who experience conflict between their careers and one or more of the 3 Ms.

Like most new graduate students, I had envisioned my dissertation as simply a culmination of my studies, a milestone to mark the earning of my degree and the return to professional life. However, in the course of doing this research, I found that this dissertation was truly just a beginning for me. As I interviewed each woman and sat with her as she talked about her story, often through tears, I was struck by how many of them confided in me that they had never before shared their painful feelings with anyone. A few asked me for copies of their interview transcripts, hoping that their conversations with me would help them finally find the words they needed to help their spouses understand them.

At the conclusion of my study, I invited all my research participants to an informal briefing over pizza to share my findings. At one point, I distributed a handout representing the 3 Ms and one woman remarked, "I'm going to post this on my refrigerator so the next time I'm feeling down I can remind myself I'm not alone and I'm not crazy." That was the moment I knew this was not the end for me. I had to find a way to keep sharing these stories to help others who were struggling with these same issues and, perhaps, suffering in silence.

Since that day, I have moved three more times – to Washington, DC, then to Hawaii, and then back to Washington, DC, again. I returned to the consulting world but made time to focus on military spouse employment. I began coaching career-oriented military spouses, contributed to new research, wrote articles and book chapters, and spoke to a variety of policy and military audiences. This book, however, is the accomplishment I am most proud of because I am finally able to share the words of so many women whom I have carried with me in my work. I hope their sincere, and often painful, words will move you the way they have moved me.

As a collection of stories, this book is not meant to be a comprehensive representation of the entire military spouse population. As I explained in my discussion of methodology, I intentionally created a sample that was homogeneous in some ways so that I could more easily draw conclusions from a smaller group. Technically speaking, I cannot generalize any of these findings beyond female Air Force spouses stationed in Germany. In particular, this study did not address the unique challenges and experiences of male military spouses, although their struggles are equally valid and deserve further investigation. Our experiences are certainly diverse in many ways, but I also believe that we, as military spouses, share a great deal in common. I hope that readers will find meaning in these stories regardless of gender, branch of service, or duty station.

Chapter 1 – Introduction

My Story

I felt like my career was over when I should have been in my prime. I was a new military spouse in my mid-30s, moving overseas for the first time, and I found myself staring at my Turkish residency permit. Although I had written "unemployed" on the occupation section of the application, I received a permit stamped with the words "Ev Hanimi," Turkish for housewife. I was devastated. These two words seemed to confirm my worst fears that my hard-earned career was a thing of the past. I wasn't simply an unemployed professional; I was now a full-time military wife, an identity I was reluctant to embrace. Any previous career success and credentials I had earned didn't seem to matter anymore. This was the moment in my marriage when I realized I could no longer pretend that the military was just my husband's job. It was now how the world saw me, whether I liked it or not.

When my husband and I first met, James was a young captain in the Air Force. At that point in my life, I had little exposure to the military, having grown up in Berkeley, California, a liberal college town known for antiwar activism. Needless to say, people in the military were about as foreign to me as aliens from another planet. My grandfather was a World War II veteran, but military service was not a consideration among my peer group of liberal-minded young adults. I suspect, like many civilians, I was happy to enjoy the benefits of a strong military, but reluctant to personally associate myself with the messy business of war fighting.

Even after James and I married, I preferred to maintain a negative stereotype of military members and spouses, assuming my husband and I were the exceptions. Preserving my own career was a vital part of my unconscious strategy to distance myself and remain outside the military at all costs and not become a *real* military spouse.

At first, I was able to maintain my career path without too much disruption. I was working for a large consulting firm that allowed me to transfer offices to accommodate military moves. But then James was selected to attend graduate school with a follow-on assignment to Turkey. My firm vaguely suggested I might be able to work out of one of our European offices if I was willing to commute to England or Germany each week, a prospect I did not find appealing.

When James was first offered this opportunity, we discussed the possibility that this might be the right time for him to leave the Air Force. Moving overseas to such a remote location seemed like the kiss of death for my career, something we had earlier agreed I would not have to sacrifice. As James considered his options, one of his commanders found out I was concerned about moving to Turkey and made a point of talking to me. Although he meant to be reassuring, this commander's words had the opposite effect. In essence, his advice was something like this: "You really shouldn't worry about going to Turkey. I hear the shopping is amazing!" I was perplexed and chagrined that he believed shopping would be a suitable replacement for my career.

In the end, we agreed that James should take the school assignment and we would go to Turkey, confirming his commitment to stay in the Air Force for several more years. Although I was anxious about the impact on my career, I also realized that my current career path was unsustainable. I liked being a consultant, but the demands of a big firm were intense and the weekly business travel was exhausting. My stress level was high enough that I had developed a cardiac arrhythmia, and the frequent palpitations were impacting both my physical and mental health. I knew I needed a change, and James was committed to continuing his military service as long as I was supportive. So, I took the plunge, quit my consulting job, and we moved to Turkey.

More than 15 years later, James is still on active duty and has served in the Air Force for 26 years. We have enjoyed nine assignments together, and now have two children, ages 8 and 12.

Throughout those moves, I have kept my consulting career going in various forms, with plenty of detours along the way. Although it has been challenging, I'm surprisingly satisfied with the work I've cobbled together as an independent consultant, coach, researcher, and writer. I earn far less than I did during my consulting firm days, but also work a fraction of the hours, and am infinitely healthier and happier. Because I took that detour from a big-firm consulting career, I also enjoyed the opportunity to go back to school and pursue the research that is the basis for this book. This research, in particular, has opened up a whole new world for me as an advocate for military spouse employment. Perhaps if I had not ended up in Turkey as an unemployed "Ev Hanimi," I never would have left my corporate career path and found the calling I'm so passionate about today.

Why This Book

My goal in writing this book is to help other spouses who have experienced similar career setbacks and to show them that they are not alone. If you are a military spouse, my hope is that you will come away feeling a little less lonely in your frustrations and that you will be able to find a framework for charting a career path that works for you. I am not going to tell you that it is easy to be a career-oriented spouse, and the reality is that the deck is stacked against us. Military life has not been designed to support our careers, regardless of how many well-intended programs attempt to mitigate this reality. We are fighting an uphill battle, but that doesn't mean you have to sacrifice absolutely everything, and you don't have to sacrifice who you are. **The message of this book is to be thoughtful about fitting the pieces of your life together into a complementary whole: your career, your marriage, your family, and your military life.** The people you will meet in this book all illustrate the power of fit, demonstrating how satisfying life can be when the pieces come together and how devastating it can be when they don't.

Throughout this research, I have been profoundly struck by the isolation these women universally express. Some have found positive ways to reconcile career and military life. Others have struggled to find a resolution or have reluctantly accepted an undesirable state of unemployment or underemployment. Many opted for motherhood as a full-time vocation, with mixed feelings about taking this path. Whether they painted their stories in a positive or negative light, what remained the same was a sense that they often felt alone in this struggle.

Despite the fact that most interview participants acknowledged that employment is a widespread challenge for military spouses, they also often felt each setback as a personal failure. As military spouses, we feel we should be smart enough, educated enough, and resilient enough to achieve our goals, yet we become despondent when our dreams do not come to fruition. And, as my participants share in their stories, we often internalize that pain (Jervis, 2011) and miss the opportunity to support each other in our common experiences.

My hope in writing this book is to reach military spouses who have embarked on this journey, and to show them they are not alone in their struggle. I wish I had known other career-oriented military spouses 18 years ago when I was daunted by the prospect of marrying into the military. I thought I was an anomaly because I had a career and wanted to keep having a career. The reality is that I am not unusual, and neither are you.

If you are not a military spouse, I hope you will appreciate these stories of sacrifice that are rarely shared in the public sphere. Moreover, there are lessons in these stories that poignantly apply to civilian women who also seek to integrate work and family life. Married working women and working mothers have traditionally borne the burden of the "second shift" (Hochschild, 2012) by doing the majority of household tasks regardless of their employment status. Military spouses represent an extreme version of this dynamic because they often carry the traditional roles of wife and mother while also navigating the complexities of military relocations, deployments, and constant military demands.

Definition of the Problem

You are in good company if you are a military spouse struggling to maintain a career, and current research on this subject reveals just how broad and deep the military spouse employment problem is. About half of all military spouses are employed at any given time. Based on a total population of 640,000 active duty spouses across all branches of service, the Department of Defense (DoD) estimated that 41% are employed in the civilian workforce, 13% are members of the armed forces, 12% are unemployed, and 34% are not in the labor force (Defense Manpower Data Center, 2015). "Unemployment" refers to those who are not working but actively seeking employment, and those "not in the labor force" are a combination of spouses who choose not to work and those who would like to work but have become discouraged from actively seeking employment. In fact, a recent survey conducted by Blue Star Families[1] (2016a) indicated that 60% of spouses not currently working would like to be employed, regardless of whether or not they are actively job searching.

Not surprisingly, an increasing number of military spouses claim that being a military spouse has negatively impacted their careers. While 66% of spouses participating in a 2004 RAND survey (Castaneda & Harrell, 2008) identified a negative impact, 79% of spouses participating in a 2016 Blue Star Families survey (2016a) responded similarly. One interpretation of this increase is that the current generation of military spouses is more likely to expect to

---

[1] Blue Star Families (BSF) is a nonprofit organization founded by military spouses to improve the quality of life for military families through a variety of programs, research, and advocacy initiatives. Their research includes the Annual Military Family Lifestyle Survey, the largest survey of military families conducted outside the DoD. For the past several years, I was a member of the BSF survey team and their subject matter expert on spouse employment.

have a career and feels more negatively impacted if that expectation is not met.

Unemployment, in particular, remains high despite recent initiatives by the federal government and the private sector to employ military spouses. One striking point of comparison is the disparity between the unemployment rate for military spouses compared to that of the general population of married adults in the United States. In 2015, the unemployment rate[2] for civilian married adults in the United States was 3% (Bureau of Labor Statistics, 2015), while the unemployment rate for all active duty military spouses was 23% (Defense Manpower Data Center, 2015), a figure more than seven times greater.

Underemployment is also pervasive among military spouses who work. A worker may be underemployed if she is in a position for which she is overqualified or underpaid, or in a position where she is not working as many hours as she would like to be. A recent survey conducted by the Institute for Veterans and Military Families found that 90% of working female military spouses claimed to be underemployed (Maury & Stone, 2014). Underemployment is created by a confluence of factors that impact military spouses: education and experience levels, the quality of jobs available near military installations, and discontinuity of employment created by frequent relocation.

Underemployment is driven largely by the fact that military spouses have higher levels of education, on average, compared to their civilian counterparts, making it more likely that they will be overqualified for available positions (Lim, Golinelli, & Cho, 2007). Economists have also concluded that military installations create a negative job market for military spouses by producing low-wage

---

[2] The "unemployment rate" represents the percentage of people *in the labor force* who are unemployed. A person is considered to be in the labor force if he or she is currently working or *actively seeking employment*. This statistic is different than the percent of spouses who are unemployed, which is calculated as a percentage of *all* spouses, whether they are in the labor force or not.

service sector jobs that an oversupply of female labor must compete for, only further depressing wages (Booth, 2003).

Finally, the fact that military families move every 2 to 3 years impacts spouse earnings significantly. Frequent relocation lies at the heart of the challenge for career-oriented spouses who find themselves following their service members from one assignment to the next. This dynamic of "tied migration" typically creates breaks in employment for the "trailing spouse," which in turn leads to significantly lower earnings and increased levels of unemployment (Cooke & Speirs, 2005). Cooke and Speirs estimated that relocation alone adds 10% to the rate of military spouse unemployment.

Overall, lower incomes earned by military spouses translates into a significant pay gap compared to civilian spouses. On average, female military spouses earn 50% of the income earned by female civilian spouses, and male military spouses earn 70% of the income earned by male civilian spouses (Hisnanick & Little, 2015; Little & Hisnanick, 2007). A survey conducted by Blue Star Families (2017) found that 52% of *all* military spouse respondents earned no income at all in the previous calendar year, while 51% of their *employed* military spouse respondents earned less than $20,000 in that same year. Not only do spouse underemployment and unemployment directly impact the financial health of military families themselves, but they also lead to significant social costs as well. Blue Star Families (2016b) calculated that military spouse unemployment and underemployment create an annual social cost of approximately $1 billion, derived from a combination of lost tax revenue that could be generated by more gainfully employed military spouses, and taxpayer money currently spent toward unemployment compensation for military spouses.

Until more workers are able to break the link between geography and employment, most military spouses will be forced to reinvent themselves with each move. Often that results in lost time in the workforce, gaps in a resume, and a patchy career path with little advancement. Those transition costs take a toll financially, as well as emotionally, when faced with the loss of one's anticipated career goals.

This dilemma created by frequent relocation needs to be understood within the broader context of military culture and gender roles. Military spouse employment remains such a sticky problem precisely because it is exacerbated by two deeply rooted and interconnected dynamics: a traditional military culture based on a single breadwinner family model, and a population of military spouses that is 92% female (Department of Defense, 2016).

When you think of the stereotype of the traditional military spouse, what image comes to mind? First, she is female and probably has children. Her primary job is to "keep the home fires burning" while her husband is protecting our nation. She is there to proudly support her husband and take care of the household so he can focus on serving his country. That is the traditional narrative that largely survives today, even though about half of all military families are dual-income households. Mady Segal (1986), a military sociologist who broke ground on this subject in the 1980s, described the military as a "greedy" institution because service members are expected to be dedicated 100% to their jobs, including the willingness to sacrifice their own lives in combat. But because that greedy mindset is part of the military culture, it is often the norm that the (male) service member dedicates all to his job, and the (female) spouse is responsible for everything on the homefront, often including expectations to contribute free labor as a volunteer within the military unit. Adding a spouse career to the mix contradicts that norm, introducing conflict within our military system and creating tension for military families.

The fact that military spouses are a predominately female population adds a gender-based dimension to employment challenges. It is still a commonly held assumption in our society that women are the primary caregivers when children are present in a family. That's not unique to the military community, but it is a norm that impacts military spouses heavily since 67% of them have children (Department of Defense, 2015). That means, in addition to the challenges presented by military life, most career-oriented military spouses also have to address the typical issues that any civilian working mom would encounter. Those issues may include access to childcare, division of household responsibilities, and the need for flexibility in employment.

In fact, military spouses have consistently identified three significant obstacles to their employment: service member job demands (including relocations and deployments), family obligations, and childcare (Blue Star Families, 2016a). There is no one silver bullet to fix these military spouse employment issues. Rather, the quest to maintain a career requires a holistic approach to integrating all the competing demands in one's life as a working military spouse. This is where my research and the stories in this book will take us.

The 3 Ms of Spouse Employment

Landing a job is only one small part of the employment challenge for military spouses. The more difficult task is *maintaining* employment when faced with a lifestyle of many competing demands. I call these competing roles the 3 Ms: Marriage, Motherhood, and Military Life. As the real-life stories in this book illustrate, the key to maintaining a satisfying and successful career is finding employment that fits with all the other primary roles in one's life.

Marriage is one experience common to all military spouses, and the nature of this partnership can either break or make a spouse's career. As the stories in Chapter 2 demonstrate, sometimes the marriage relationship can have an extremely positive or negative impact while, for others, it is a subtle, contributing factor. Those spouses who are able to achieve a successful career path often have partners who support them in their efforts, either through encouragement, the sharing of household responsibilities, or both.

Motherhood also plays a primary role for the majority of military spouses. The stories from my research are motherhood stories, but the same principle applies to fathers as well. That is, a military spouse's career plans must fit his or her expectations and demands as a parent if he or she is going to maintain a career that will be satisfying and sustainable. For many spouses, self-expectations of good parenting are obstacles to reentering the workforce or become sources of conflict upon returning to work. Chapter 3 offers a range of different parenting scenarios, demonstrating the ways in which military spouses reconcile the demands of mothering and career aspirations.

Military Life, the last M, is perhaps the factor that receives the most attention when discussing military spouse employment. In addition to juggling parenting and partner expectations, a military spouse has the additional demand of navigating the complexities of military life. For the typical spouse, that means relocating every few years (often to overseas locations), as well as coping with service member deployments, demanding or unpredictable schedules, and time spent away from home for temporary duty (TDY). Combined with a high operations tempo, and a traditional expectation that a spouse pitch in and volunteer to assist the service member's unit, military life can become a serious career obstacle to many military spouses. Chapter 4 highlights these experiences through the stories of spouses who have been significantly impacted by military life.

Ultimately, solutions to the problem of military spouse employment cannot simply focus on the challenges of military life in isolation, but must include the impact of all 3 Ms experienced cumulatively. For some, the combination is deadly and careers grind to a halt. Others find ways to compromise and achieve a career that accommodates the other demands in their lives. Those that express the greatest level of satisfaction are the ones who mindfully manage all 3 Ms and find the best fit between their careers and their life situations. Chapter 5 includes stories of spouses who have skillfully integrated the 3 Ms to forge satisfying career paths.

The final chapter of this book concludes with thoughts about possible, meaningful solutions for the future on a systemic level. Although reconciling the 3 Ms may be a useful coping strategy in the short term, it is not a long-term remedy to a complex, systemic problem deeply imbedded in military culture and policy. Chapter 6 looks at the root causes of the spouse employment conundrum, and outlines potential ways to move the needle on such an intractable problem.

Chapter 2 – Marriage

You might be wondering why you picked up a book about careers and now find yourself reading about marriage. By definition, all military spouses have a partner in marriage. And, of course, all marriages are uniquely wonderful as well as uniquely flawed. No relationship is perfect, and the purpose of this book is not to evaluate or judge the health of your marriage. Rather, the point here is that your marriage is one important factor to take into account when you are planning your career, because the support you do or don't receive from your spouse may make all the difference in the world in being able to sustain that career.

The stories in this book are excerpts from interviews I conducted with real military spouses, although I have given them fictitious names to protect their identities. Each of these stories paints a picture of a unique life experience, with all the complexity and contradiction that is part of real life. As such, the stories in this chapter speak to a variety of topics, not just the individual's marriage. However, the stories I selected for this chapter illustrate key points about the challenges and opportunities a career-oriented military spouse might encounter in her marriage. As you will find, these women share their very personal ups and downs with employment challenges and the ways in which their marriages helped or hindered them at various points.

Brenda is frustrated that her husband is not more supportive of her efforts to go back to work long after she intended to reenter the workforce. She feels they are entrenched in their respective roles: his as the singularly focused Air Force pilot and hers as the one who keeps the household running. Trying to fit a job into her life feels impossible because her husband still expects her to maintain the household single-handedly, just as she has always done. She seems to accept her fate as inevitable, claiming that the Air Force is her husband's "excuse job" that prevents him from taking on any real responsibility at home.

Serena's views about marriage have evolved since becoming a military spouse. She stresses how important it was for her to be independent after watching her mother's failed relationships with men. And her frustration with being unemployed is related, in part, to this desire to be independent and self-sufficient. But now, she says she is "growing up" and realizes that marriage is about partnership, not the needs of two separate people. Reframing that definition of marriage helps her feel more secure that she is contributing to their partnership in ways that can't be measured by her earnings. She also feels reassured that her husband is comfortable with her not working, and together they are making plans to start a family.

Lisa claims that being able to maintain her independence is central to her marriage. Being able to make a financial contribution to the family by working is essential, and she has been creative in finding alternative ways to do so when her dream of becoming a commercial pilot slowly drifted away. Something in her marriage seems to have shifted over the years as well. While they originally agreed that she would become the primary breadwinner when her husband retires from the military, as that time approaches, they both realize that she has not yet established the career she hoped for, making it less practical to make her the primary earner. And although Lisa has made career sacrifices for her husband's military moves and deployments, *he* has been reluctant to endure geographic separation for the sake of *her* career.

Kendra has experienced a change in her marriage since she separated from active duty herself and became a civilian military spouse. She worries about maintaining her own financial independence, and says her husband doesn't understand her civilian experience or her complaints about not being able to find employment. Kendra has taken on more household chores that they used to share, which she finds unsatisfying. She hopes her husband wants more for her, but suspects he would like for her to stay home and be a housewife, like many other spouses they know.

18

Nicole says her husband's support has been critical to her career. He is not only supportive in spirit, but shoulders his share of childcare and family responsibilities, picking up the slack when she is required to travel or work long hours. He has even offered to leave the military and allow her career to take priority. However, Nicole is not comfortable being the primary breadwinner and wants to maintain a supportive role, preserving the option to stay home with her children when she chooses to. Knowing she and her husband are partners in this decision opens up many possibilities.

Felice is a newlywed openly questioning the viability of juggling two marriages: one to her husband and one to the military. She feels defeated by her efforts to find suitable employment, and already foresees a negative impact on her marriage if she is unable to get back on her feet. Felice's frustrations seem to have a snowball effect, where concerns about employment have led to insecurities about self-worth, the health of her marriage, and, ultimately, her long-term happiness as a military spouse.

Michelle Still Mehta

Brenda

"Establish the way you want it to be before you get married. Don't mow the lawn if you don't plan to mow the lawn for the next 40 years."

Brenda has been a military spouse for 14 years and is the mother of three school-age children. She first met her husband while working in Germany as an accountant for an American company. She looks back on that time and marvels at how brave and independent she was to move to Germany all on her own after graduating from college. After meeting her husband, she followed him to an assignment in New Jersey, where they married. She continued to work as an accountant during that assignment until her son was born and they prepared to move to Scott Air Force Base, Illinois.

I got married at 30. I had worked all my life. It wasn't ever really a consideration that I not work. I had worked through school, worked hard, was a CPA [certified public accountant]. I paid a lot of money for school loans, and was still paying them off, so [work] was important to me. I didn't know any different. It was an automatic thing to go find a job. I mean, it was pretty normal as to what everyone else in the world does.

But when I had my son, I stopped working altogether. We were getting ready to move anyway, and you have a new baby, and you don't know what you're doing. So it worked out at that point. We both thought it was important, and it didn't hurt us not to work at that time, because I was going to quit soon anyway because of the move [to Scott Air Force Base].

Back then, it felt like [I had options]. I don't think there are very many mothers of newborn babies that want to go back to work right away. It does feel like you're essentially being gifted something. Especially with my background, working my way through college, and then working the whole time, it did feel like kind of a gift. It was nice not to have to go back to work. Financially, yes, of course,

20

more money would have been nice. But it wasn't the most important thing at that time. So it did kind of feel luxurious. I had options in that it wasn't necessary for me to go right back to work after I had my son.

I was thinking, "Well, I'll stay home for 5 years. When my son goes to kindergarten, then I'll go back to work, and I'll go back on my thing." That's what everyone I knew did or had to do. So I think that was my mindset. Okay, I'll have kids. And because of that mindset, I had my son. And then directly after that, we had decided that we wanted to have another child. And I said, "Well, it has to be now because I have 5 years." Maybe I can stretch it to 6, but we got pregnant right away and we had twins. So I had three kids within 18 months and I was thinking the way I had always thought: "When these kids were in kindergarten, I was going back to work."

When I found out we were going to Scott [Air Force Base], I wasn't terribly excited about it. I didn't even try to work in Illinois because I knew it was impossible, just having the kids. So I think that was the biggest assignment that – not devastated me – but it kind of changed me. Not only did we move to Scott, but we ended up moving on base. I had never been around the military, so it was kind of a culture shock. And I remember living on base and my girlfriend saying one time, "Oh, you're one of those people. You live on base. You shop at that base grocery store. Your kids are going to go to that base school." I mean, that was kind of shocking to me because I always envisioned myself as this really open-minded, free spirit. I'll try anything. And then, all of a sudden, I'm in my small world. My identity changed, or what I thought my identity was.

When we left New Jersey [for Scott Air Force Base], that was my first thought, "Why do you even try to work, because we're only going to be there for 2½ years?" You can't get anywhere in 2½ years. You can't progress. Who wants to hire me for 2½ years? I'm not going to lie and say that we're going to be here for 6 years, because that's not how you do business. So it changes your mindset; and it changes your motivation, because, really, can you do all these things that in your mind you built up for yourself? I mean, you can, if you want to hit your head against the wall. I was kind of disheartened. It's kind of like it doesn't matter how hard I try in this arena, I'm not going to get anywhere.

No matter how many people tell you that motherhood is noble and good and all that, you still have it in your mind like, "Yeah, right. I should be doing something more." I think we always want to see the fruits of it. When you go to work you get the paycheck. You get the accolade. When you stay home, you don't get any of that, not in the short term. You get it when you have great kids at the end. But when your kids are screaming in Walmart and you've tried your best and you're doing everything possible, you just don't see. When you clean the house perfectly spic and span and in half an hour it's just as crazy as when you started, you just don't have those cues that you're doing a good job, or that you're doing anything really.

At work, people are looking at you to do your job. And when you're at home, you're trying to get people to look at you. People [at the office] are constantly critiquing your work or looking at your work or praising your work or criticizing your work. They're always looking. But when you're at home, you're trying to get someone to acknowledge that you're doing something of worth, but no one's looking. Maybe your husband looks every once in a while. Maybe your mother-in-law looks every once in a while. But, really, no one's looking.

Brenda talks about the early years of motherhood as a mixed blessing. She appreciates the gift of being able to make the choice to stay home, and says it's almost a luxury to have that opportunity. But she is also candid about the downside she has felt, doing the work of caregiving that is often invisible or unrecognized by anyone else. Although her choice to stay home is a positive one during her children's preschool years, she becomes increasingly frustrated as her kids get older and she still finds the prospect of going back to work untenable. Once her children reach the kindergarten years, she is determined to work at least part time, but encounters repeated roadblocks in her attempts to go back to work. When she moves to Andrews

Air Force Base, Maryland, Brenda takes a retail job at Williams-Sonoma, working 15 hours a week, but finds that it is too difficult to carve out the time she needs. Later, she takes a job stocking Hallmark cards in grocery stores, which is meant to be a flexible, 10-hour-per-week position, but even that was too much.

Brenda's frustration begins to take a toll on her marriage as well. Here, she describes her feelings of growing resentment toward her husband because his job as an Air Force pilot has become the universal "excuse job" that exonerates him from household responsibilities and shifts the burden of "picking up all the stuff" to Brenda.

Our husbands have such interesting jobs. No matter what their job is, they are well traveled. They're doing something interesting and brave and noble. And not that you're competing, but that's always very interesting to people. Nobody's really interested in how many diapers you changed. When you're not working, I think a lot of people assume that you have nothing to say or nothing to offer. I got tired of that too. It's like, "Where did you fly today?" or "How is it down in Abu Dhabi or Djibouti?" All these exotic, interesting places that no one gets to see or know about. And then, "Brenda, how was the mall today?"

[During] the first assignment, I didn't know [what military life would be like]. I knew that we moved, but I didn't realize about the jobs; and I didn't realize about my changing. That was just dumb on my part. I mean, you realize that things are going to change. But I really didn't know. This is really hard. I always thought that I was a really strong person. I moved to Germany by myself [before I was married]. I'm independent. I'm fine. And yeah, I think it's hard. It's harder than anybody can imagine.

I have a little bit of resentment. I mean, there's just no question. It always falls to me. There's no question of who's going to take care of everything, who's going to get the dishwasher fixed, who's going to do all those things. I don't even ask my husband anymore. If something's broken in the house, I figure it out. If I need something moved, I figure out how to move it. I don't wait, because I get frustrated waiting. I'm sure it hurts my husband's feelings, but I always tell him, "I can't depend on you. I can't wait for you, because then I'm just too frustrated. I get upset because you've been gone. For example, I've been wanting to move this piece of furniture that's too heavy for me, so I've waited for 4 months. And now you're home and you're still too tired or jet lagged for 2 more weeks to move it." So there's just not a question of who it's going to fall to. It's always going to fall to me, because he has this excuse job. It gets him off of any responsibility at home until he wants to jump back in. I don't have a choice to jump out and in. I always have to be the leveling figure, the one that makes everything happen and everything smooth at home. And not that that's bad, but there's no chance of me getting a real job or a career.

The Andrews assignment is where my twins went to kindergarten. In my mind, they were in kindergarten, so I was going to try to do a little something, but the Williams-Sonoma job was the hardest job I've ever had. And it was not because of the work. It was because I was trying to figure out how to squeeze it all in. I was trying to figure out how to still do all of my stuff that I needed to do [at home] because it's established that I do all these things now. I cook, clean, garden, take care of the kids, do the homework, and all these things. That's my established role at this point. And now I'm adding 15 whole hours a week, but it was very hard. It was very hard to put those little hours in. Even though the kids are in school, that 15 hours a week takes away from all those responsibilities that I'm in charge of, because he is working. So those 15 hours a week took away from "picking up the stuff."

It was devastating to think that I can't [do all of this]. I mean, in my mind, I'm thinking, "Are you kidding? I used to work 60 hours a week." It's devastating to think that I don't even have 15 hours a week that I could pursue something, [and] that all of my efforts go to the care and support of other people. That's okay, but at some point, you wish that you had some support. Everyone talks about, "Oh, you guys make great money in the military." But it's not great money if it doesn't allow me to have a job. So you're paying for two people really. It changes my whole attitude and my belief in what's possible. It's very sad for me that I can't do anything really.

Brenda begins to cry...

It's frustrating. Like, the Hallmark job, all I had to do was place cards in the slots in the grocery store and order more cards. I think those [retail] jobs were something to do, to talk to people and get out and see what was going on after being with babies for 5 years. And the frustrating thing is that doing even these little jobs wasn't possible. That was the devastating part.

I was angry that my husband – and his pursuing everything for our country – didn't leave me 10 hours a week to place cards in slots. I think that's what it comes down to. It's always feeling like you have to be the one in charge, or the one that does everything for your family to the point that you can't have a little 10-hour-a-week job. That's the issue that I have with my husband, not that he can do anything about it.

Brenda's emotions are raw during our interview, especially as she begins to bring her story up to their present assignment in Germany. Her children are now well beyond their kindergarten years, the milestone at which she had planned to return to work, but she has been unable to do so. Upon arriving in Germany, an acquaintance with a real estate business approaches Brenda's husband about a potential job for her, knowing that Brenda speaks German and has professional skills. He thought Brenda would be a good fit in his real estate company, and Brenda's husband encourages her to give it a try. Although she loves the job, her return to work has made it more challenging for Brenda to keep up with all the "stuff" in the household that she is responsible for. As a result, Brenda's husband has asked her to resign and she has agreed to quit her new job. Brenda shares what this episode has been like and what she takes away from this experience.

After the Andrews assignment, I had pretty much given up. I had pretty much said, "I'm not working again." I've tried and I've tried, but I finally got to the point where I just said [to my husband], "Okay, I'm not able to work. That's the bottom line. I can't work with your job, so I'm not going to try anymore. I'm not going to

25

bang my head against the wall. I'm not going to get frustrated about this anymore. It is on you. So when you retire, you get another job because I'm done. I'm done working. I can't go up and down anymore." My husband was fine with that.

But, he has a friend here [in Germany], from when we lived here the first time, who has a [real estate] company. And my husband said, "Oh, [my friend] has a job. Do you want it?" So I'm like, "Sure, that's fine, that's great. Maybe this job won't be as demanding and maybe I can actually do this job." I speak German, so that was perfect. I started working in January, and it's a busy job. I mean, it's a very busy job. My kids are now in fourth and fifth grade, so I was thinking they should be a little bit more independent. I have a telephone from 9:00 a.m. to 6:00 p.m. that I answer, and I work from 9:00 a.m. to 3:00 p.m. I really like it. It's one of those things where it's fulfilling. I talk to different people. I get to do some marketing. It's really a great job, but my husband still sees my role as that support role. When his parents come, and he's on a trip for work, I'm still the one responsible for taking care of everyone when they come. So when you have people coming every 2 weeks, and he's getting deployed for 6 months, there's just no way for me to do a job.

How did you come to the point of deciding you couldn't keep this job?

It wasn't my decision. I think my husband is so used to me being around and not working that he really doesn't want me to [continue working]. I mean, he really doesn't like it.

Even though this job was his idea in the first place?

It's the reality of me working every day, having a phone, and not everything in our house being perfect, because it's not anymore. The floor's not always mopped because I'm working. Then I pick up the kids and we do homework and we go to baseball. Then we come home and I throw something together for dinner. So we've had a lot of problems because he doesn't like it. It's not running the way he thinks it should run. And he's a good guy. He's totally not like one of those 1960s guys, but I think it's been established through our marriage. And it's different now because he's never had to do anything. He's never, not once, cooked a meal. He does other things, but he's never been in our kitchen.

It's so stressful. Obviously, it's easier if I don't do [the job], because I'm doing a lot. I'm working very hard at home with the kids and at work because our life has determined that my husband doesn't have any role in our home life and the running of it. So it hasn't changed. I've just added a job. So I am tired. I remember someone said when I got married, "Establish the way you want it to be before you get married. Don't mow the lawn if you don't plan to mow the lawn for the next 40 years." Now I wish I had listened to this tidbit of advice. And it's frustrating for me. But now I really, truly feel as if my role is to be the support, to make sure that my husband gets someplace in his career, wherever he wants to go, and that my kids get wherever they want to go in their lives, which is what I would want to do for my kids anyway. But somehow, with the husband thing, I'm getting a little bit more and more resentful as I see that it's so one sided. There's that expectation through the years that we promote his career to my nonpromotion of anything I want to do. And I love him. He's a great man. He's a really good guy. It's just the establishment of the life. You do what you have to do to make it work. And that's what it's always had to be.

I just don't feel like I've had any control over the development of my life. It's just like I said. You just follow and do what you have to do to make everything work. And you don't have really any say or any play with where you can go or what you can do. You feel limited.

I don't know if I have energy [for working anymore]. I really think I'm just exhausted. I think I've banged my head against the wall. And I think that, at this point, 15 years later, it would take so much energy to get back into something, that I don't know if I have the energy after promoting his career [for so long]. I'm tired. I'm exhausted and I don't have anything to show for it *personally*. I mean *we* do. We always used to laugh at those women that wore their husband's rank or whatever. But now I'm thinking, "She worked just as hard at it as he did, so why shouldn't she?" Not that

I'd ever do that because it's kind of weird. But I can see how it happens, especially those commanders' wives. My experience with not doing what I wanted to do work wise was because of our family situation. But there are those women that don't do what they could be doing work wise because of their husband's career. And I don't know why they wouldn't wear their husband's rank. It's not an easy life. I mean, I'd still choose it because I love him, but hmmm... Would it have been a bad thing if he was a doctor or an electrical engineer? I don't know.

Brenda's story is a painful illustration of the importance of shared expectations within a marriage. Although Brenda was glad to stay home and be a full-time caregiver when her children were young, she found it hard to extract herself from this role later in life. Not only did she feel the burden of juggling career and household responsibilities when she tried to return to work, but her husband was unwilling to live with the impact the change had on him. Interestingly, there seemed to be no real discussion about how he could help or pick up the slack at home in order to support Brenda's desire to work. While there is no formula for a good marriage or the right division of roles, it is essential that both parties agree to whatever arrangement they find suitable. In Brenda's case, the role that worked for her when her three children were babies does not work for her now that her children are in elementary school. Right or wrong, the fact that Brenda and her husband have different expectations for the household make it nearly impossible for her to pursue a career without damaging her marriage. Just like people, marriages can and do evolve and change as partnerships. The challenge for Brenda will be to navigate the next phase of her marriage and decide whether she is willing to remain in the role that has been established, or renegotiate roles with her husband in a way that will allow them both to thrive and be happy.

Serena

"I still want to be independent, but marriage isn't really about separate people."

Serena is a new military spouse at her first duty station, and also a recent college graduate. Although Serena's marriage is still in its early years, she has already encountered many challenges starting out. Serena and her husband first met as college students, where she planned to begin a career in editing. He was forced to drop out of college because he could not afford to continue. Serena describes their financial challenges before they got married, when they were simply trying to cobble together multiple low-wage jobs to eke out a living. She explains that her husband's decision to enlist in the Air Force offered financial stability that they might not have otherwise enjoyed.

[After graduating] I had a library job and a bookstore job. And then my boyfriend [now husband] had a pizza job and a library job. So we had four jobs together just to make ends meet. We were barely making it at that point. That's one of the huge reasons he decided to join the Air Force, because we knew it was just a lot more secure.

[I wanted] more security because, [with] part time, you don't have any benefits – no health benefits or anything like that. So it was hard. I didn't really go to the doctor because then you had to pay out of pocket. [I just wanted] to have a little bit more money so we could have more than $100 left over for the month, to live comfortably. I mean, that's the majority of what I was looking for.

I guess it was a little bit frustrating because I wanted one job. I wanted a nine-to-five job, [so I could] come home, relax, and not have to worry about my job. But I was really too busy to do anything. And we didn't have a car at the time. We lived 10 miles away from where we were working, so you had to take the bus, but the bus system wasn't that great. There were only specific times you could go, so he would go sleep over at his brother's house

29

sometimes during the week so he could work at the pizza shop. There was a lot of time we couldn't spend together. I didn't like that.

When I went to college, I thought, "Hey, I'll actually find an editing job when I get out of school." No, I was just happy not to be working at McDonald's. I mean, I wasn't quite happy, and I definitely wasn't content, but I was okay with working in the library at the time because I thought, eventually, I'll get to where I want to go. I haven't quite gotten there yet. And, at this point, I'm not even sure I want to be an editor anymore, but at least I was doing some freelance. At least I was doing something.

I never really wanted to be a military wife. I didn't grow up in the military or anything like that, but my mom moved a lot when we were kids. I didn't really want that for my kids. I guess by then I was okay with moving because I'd done it so much, but I just wanted my kids to stay in one place, make lifetime friends, something stable.

I was in love with him, though, and I was not going to break up with him because he joined the military. That's just silly. So I was okay with him joining. I supported him either way that he went. Actually, it was a very smart decision, and I'm completely okay with it now.

I don't have to worry about my health now. Before he joined the military, we had no coverage. Now I don't have to worry about not calling the doctor because I don't have money, which is a huge relief. And he makes enough money to support both of us. We don't have to work four or five part-time jobs together to get $100 left over [at the end of the month]. So I'm not worried about food. I'm not worried about anything like that, which, again, is a huge relief because I'm no longer stressed about it. The only thing I worried about was finding a job, which I don't even have to now. So, I feel like I'm getting to be lazy.

Supporting her husband's decision to enlist in the Air Force was a seminal point in Serena's marriage. Although she says she didn't want to be a military wife and all that entails, she decided that financial security trumped any other concerns she may have had. It was only when they arrived at their first duty station in Germany that her career aspirations were tested. After job searching for several months, she began to realize that she may have to change her expectations.

[When we got to Germany] I looked for at least 6 months trying to find jobs. I mean, it is really important for me, because I'm used to being independent. I'm not used to relying on anybody, and it was actually hard to sit at home as a housewife and not work. I feel like I should contribute somehow because my mom took care of her four kids all by herself. She worked to support us, and it's just weird to rely on my husband. I'm getting used to it now. I know I can do it now. But at the beginning, I thought, "I need to work. I need to help contribute."

Being independent was important. My mom taught me to be independent. She also hasn't had the greatest luck with men, so it was new [for me] to be married. I'm not used to a man taking care of me. I need to take care of myself, so I wanted to work. Then it took a while for me to be okay with him supporting me, which he is now. It's nice to be able to rely on somebody, but at the same time it was weird.

I felt guilty for not working because he was supporting me. But I've gone through that, and I talked to him about it. He's okay with me not working because we're not struggling. And we're planning on having kids soon; I know that I want to be at home for my kids. I don't really want to have them in daycare while I'm at work for 8 hours or whatever. So that's why I'm looking for freelance work, too, so I could be at home and do it.

If [my husband] wasn't okay with me not working, I probably would still be very adamant about looking for a job. I still want to be independent, but marriage isn't really about separate people. It's you working together, so it's not like I'm not contributing in my own way. I mean, I still contribute at the house and in our relationship so I don't have to work to make it a contribution. I'm just growing up.

31

Michelle Still Mehta

Serena's point of view seems to have evolved over the short time she has been married. Based on her experience growing up, she entered her marriage believing in the importance of maintaining her independence. Seeing her mother struggle in failed relationships, she believed it was important to maintain her own career. But now, Serena says her understanding of marriage is evolving. Perhaps she can still be an equal contributor to the household without being employed. As long as she and her husband agree that she does not have to work, then she is comfortable that they are on the same page and working together to build a household and a family together.

While Serena's narrative about her new outlook on home life helps her turn her attention toward starting a family, she is still a bit ambivalent about the career she might have had or may still want. However, her unrealized career cannot be fully attributed to military life or living in Germany. The confluence of various events (working multiple jobs, moving, getting married, anticipating a family and future moves) have left her feeling confused about what her aspirations actually are and what is possible for her.

I think part of the problem is I don't really know what I want to do anymore. I was looking so long for an editing job. I actually want to edit fiction [for a] publishing company. But, right now, I don't really know what I want to do. I had a goal, but I don't know anymore. Do I still want to be an editor? Do I want to go back to school? I enjoyed accounting, but I don't want to spend another $30,000 to change my career field. And, at the same time, I'm getting back into writing, and I'm enjoying that.

I think the problem here is I don't know where to go to find my specific career field. I don't know what website to look at or where to go to find these types of jobs. And that's the biggest problem. If I was in the states, there are so many different websites you can go to find stateside jobs. But here [in Germany], I only knew of two websites, and neither one of them had my career [field]. So I don't know what to do. I just don't know where to look, so I don't look anymore.

I think it's probably a little bit more difficult to be in the Air Force looking for my job. If you can get freelance jobs, it doesn't matter where you are. But if you're trying to find an actual location, work in an actual company, it's more difficult because you're constantly moving. We haven't moved yet, but I know it's coming.

It's not as bad as I thought it would be, though. Originally, I didn't really want to be a military wife, but there are some perks and there are some downsides. And I think the perks probably outweigh it, you know? It's not a bad way to live. It's not like I thought it would be originally.

I feel like I'm getting to be lazy, though, because I'm not working anymore. He was deployed for 6 months and I don't drive. It mostly comes down to not being able to drive. It's not as easy to go out. So I'm just staying at home and playing on the computer; and I read a lot. I have been getting into writing lately, which is good, so it's getting a little bit better. But I'm just not doing as much, so I feel lazy. [I feel] stir crazy, stuck in the house, and I just want to go out and do something.

At the end of Serena's interview, I am struck by her continued ambivalence. Although she is satisfied that she and her husband are making good decisions together, Serena still seems a bit out of sorts due to feeling isolated and unoccupied. She wants to believe she is doing the right thing, but still needs a sense of purpose and meaning in her daily life, something she may find in starting a family. In the meantime, she is searching for ways to pass the time and may continue to question her career decisions and aspirations. Whether or not Serena decides to explore her career options, it will be critical for her to continue making these decisions together with her husband. Just as she was instrumental in supporting his choice to enlist in the Air Force, he will need to actively help Serena navigate the choices ahead of her.

Michelle Still Mehta

Lisa

"It didn't quite come down to the marriage or the job, but there was a potential that it was going that way, and it was just not sustainable."

Lisa is originally from England and met her husband 12 years ago at a British test pilot school. When they first got married, her goal was to become a commercial pilot and gain enough experience that she could be the primary breadwinner when her husband retired from the military. In the early years of their marriage, Lisa focused on this goal, completing her schooling and becoming a pilot for small private companies. She also did some bartending along the way to earn a little extra money, preserve her sense of independence, and do something fun. Flying is Lisa's passion, and she explains that it is an "enormous amount of fun." She also says that it is rewarding to be able to do something that not many other women get to do.

I was 19 when we moved and I got married, so I probably wasn't thinking a great deal at all in some ways. But my career plan at the time was to fly commercially. So one of the attractions was really to finish my licenses, qualify, and fly for a living. And my husband had this expectation that he'd do another 10 years or so and then he'd retire and I'd be making enough money to [support] both of us. Of course, that really didn't work out. When I arrived in California, I couldn't work. I didn't have the paperwork, the work permit, and that sort of thing. I spent most of the time that I was there focused on training, looking toward being qualified to fly for a living.

I think we'd been there about 8 months when I got the work permit. And, as I started looking around, there wasn't [much]. I could have worked just to have some money. It would have been retail, that sort of thing. Also, knowing that we were at least halfway through the time we were going to spend there – we were only there for 18 months.

It was hard in the sense of independence. I've never liked the idea of not working and, therefore, being dependent for money. My mother has always worked. My grandmother always worked. It's just something that I've got a mental block about. I've never really been comfortable with it, so that was difficult. We didn't need money to maintain a household or anything like that. But it's an independence thing. I've always had an issue with not being able to work at the times that I couldn't.

Like Serena, Lisa highly values her independence and this is at the heart of her desire to maintain employment. She goes on to explain how her thinking has been shaped by her upbringing, with the belief that everyone should contribute by working in some way. Generating some income also eases any guilt she might feel about spending money that she didn't earn herself.

I went back to school, and that helped because that was me doing something constructive with my time rather than just sitting at home, really doing nothing very much but keeping house. I don't have any issues with people that choose to do that. It just doesn't work for me. I just didn't feel like I was being productive.

I grew up in quite a socialist background. So I feel that if I'm going to be getting something from the Air Force…you get all your medical care and everything like that taken care of…that I ought to be putting something back in some way. And, of course, if you're working, you're paying taxes or you are contributing in some way, even if it's not a direct route. You are contributing back into the system.

[When we went to Alabama] I took a job bartending in a restaurant, which I loved. It was a lot of fun. It was very easy. I mean, it was not something I had to put a lot of effort into, but I could earn a bit of money. If I decided I wanted a new pair of jeans or something, I didn't have to think about it. It gave me that independence to do that. So it was a regular bit of income that gave me something to do while I was still studying at home in between. It was a little bit strange when my husband's colleagues came in. An officer's wife bartending is probably a little bit strange to some people. But I was enjoying myself and that was more important. While we were there, I did actually finish my commercial license for the FAA [Federal Aviation Administration]. And I did start flying for money, but it was [only] 4 or 5 hours a week.

[When we got to Florida] I started flying full time. We could be gone from 6:00 a.m. on a Monday morning to 10:00 p.m. on a Friday night, and we'd fly every day in between. So that was almost the ideal. That was really what I wanted. I mean, it was tiring. It was hard work, but the flying itself was fantastic.

I suppose, at a very basic level, I don't think I've ever gotten out of an aircraft without a smile on my face at the end of the day. I suppose some of it's independence, some of it's the achievement of a challenge. And it's just simply fun.

I wasn't making a lot of money. By flying hours I was probably just about making minimum wage. But it was another step closer to where we thought we wanted to be. It was an achievement…that I wanted to keep going.

Being able to "fly for money" was gratifying to Lisa. She began to realize a career as a commercial pilot in Florida, and describes the satisfaction she felt to be doing something she loved. Even though the pay was low, she felt like she had reached a milestone in accomplishing her dreams, a plan that was soon derailed when they moved to Paris.

[Then we] left for Paris and we knew it was [only going to be for] 18 months. We assumed it was 18 months and back to the states. So, knowing how complicated and expensive and difficult it was, I had decided that I was not going to try and get European licenses and try to fly. So I decided that I would just find something else to do for 18 months until we got back to the states and I'd pick up more or less where I left off. As it turns out, some years later, we are still here [in Europe].

And were you still thinking that your husband would be done in a few years and you would be the breadwinner?

I think that was probably changing a little bit, partly because he wasn't showing that many signs of wanting to retire and get out. And I wasn't progressing in experience quite fast enough to be in that position for him to be able to retire completely and do nothing, if he wanted to do that.

[Flying] was still something I always thought I would go back to one way or another. But I was prepared to supplement with a second career or a parallel career at the same time. I suppose I was realizing that it wasn't going to be absolutely everything in one career forever. It was just sort of an acceptance that things don't always go the way you planned when you were 19 or 20 years old; and life puts other challenges in the way. And you sort of deal with everything as it comes along and adapt. It wasn't a dramatic thing. It was sort of a slow realization. So I don't think it was a huge impact emotionally.

Lisa is stoic in her reflection here. Although she could be heartbroken that she did not continue her career as a pilot, instead she chalks it up to life not turning out the way she planned. She accepts that life includes compromise, and this is a compromise she has made for the sake of her marriage.

After the Paris assignment, Lisa's husband deployed for a year and she went home to England. Upon her husband's return, they moved to Brussels, Belgium. She describes the employment she found with an aviation contractor in Belgium as an example of compromise. She says the job "wasn't quite real," indicating it wasn't exactly her ideal career, but it did come with a real salary that made her feel accomplished and "grown up."

I suppose I saw it as a little bit of a compromise. It wasn't flying, but it was still in the right field. It was still experience, and it was still relevant. So it wasn't quite real, but it was close enough. It was still something that was interesting. I suppose, in many ways, it was the first job that was a genuine salary. We actually did live off my salary because [I was paid in Euros] and then you didn't get into the issue of converting dollars to Euros.

That was a real achievement. It sounds ridiculous, but at 28 or 29 [years old], that felt grown up. That was real independence and productivity, being grown up and doing adult work that wasn't just part time. It wasn't working for minimum wage. It wasn't working just for expenses. This was for real. And that was good. It really was. It was a real contribution to things.

Being the stay-at-home wife, housekeeper, and, potentially, mother was never, ever going to be an option for me. I just couldn't do it. In some ways, that never changed; and this filled that [need] in probably the biggest way than anything else had because, as I say, it was a real salary. It was real, full-time work, 8:00 to 5:00, Monday to Friday, every day. So that really did feel like a proper achievement.

Lisa's feelings about achievement and contribution are highlighted here once again. She is proud of being able to independently contribute to her household and to society. Her compromise to stay in aviation without flying has served her well, and she wants to maintain her position when her husband is reassigned from Brussels to Germany.

When we [got the Germany assignment], my husband came down to Ramstein first. My husband moved down here in March. And we agreed that he would move. I would leave our house in Brussels and [instead] take a small apartment [there]. I would basically commute weekly to start with. And we would try that for a year to see out the end of my contract. Well, I was okay with it. He was not.

We gave it a good shot and decided it just wasn't worth the stress. I was driving back up [to Brussels from Germany] on Sunday nights, so I didn't even have a whole weekend down here. I was leaving before 5:00 in the evening to get back up there. So, we just decided it's not worth it for us to go through that, and I simply resigned.

I didn't want to [quit]. I loved the job. I loved the people. Again, it was sort of facing reality. It didn't quite come down to the marriage or the job, but there was a potential that it was going that way, and it was just not sustainable. It was easier for me possibly because my parents did it when I was growing up. My father was gone 4 days a week. So, for me, it was fairly normal. But my husband was adamant. "I did not marry you to live in two separate cities for 4 or 5 days every week. That's not what I wanted this life to be." I didn't really want to do it, but, again, it was sort of pragmatism and facing reality.

But my team boss came back to me the next day and she said, "If we can rewrite the contract to allow you to work from home, will you stay?" And I said, "Right, I'll stay! You just tell me what you need from me to rewrite the contract and I'll take it." So she called the company and said this is what we're proposing and they said, "Great, fine." So now I drive up [to Brussels] 4 days a month. I do 2 days every 2 weeks and just work the rest from home. And that was the deal we came to and it's worked fantastically for…a little over a year it's been.

Lisa was fortunate to work out a flexible work arrangement with her employer that allowed her to keep her job and telecommute. Ironically, she came very close to sacrificing a good job because her husband disliked being apart during the week, even though she had endured the year-long separation caused by his recent military deployment. Although we did not explore this issue further in our interview, I came away with a sense that Lisa was expected to be the more flexible party in the relationship. This dynamic has the potential to be problematic in the long run if Lisa continues to be the one to compromise on career decisions.

At the end of our interview, Lisa sums up her thoughts on being a career-oriented spouse. She laments the slow progression of her own career, but also advocates accepting reality for what it is.

You are very much on your own if you want a career. Maybe it's easier if you teach or [if] you're a nurse or something that's easily transferable. I don't know. It's been a challenge. I would like to have been further on in a career. I probably would have been if we hadn't moved, but that's reality. If you marry into the military, to a point, you just have to accept it. You can fight the system, but the system is not going to change for just a few people…If you marry into the military, it's not a stable life.

Kendra

"If you don't have a job and he decides you're not important and leaves, then what? It's easier to take care of yourself."

Kendra is an Air Force veteran trying to make sense of her military experience as well as her current role as a "dependent" military spouse.[3] She notices that her marriage has changed since she separated from active duty. She has lost some of her independence and identity that she took for granted as a service member, and is frustrated that she is now expected to take on the majority of household tasks. She worries that her husband would like her to be a housewife like other spouses they know, but feels vulnerable depending on him. After trying several different jobs over the years, Kendra says she is really a "job person" rather than a "career person." Now she is preparing to start a new job as a civilian employee in the very shop where she worked as an airman and experienced harassment as one of the few women in the unit. Kendra begins her story at the beginning, by talking about the struggles she faced as a 19-year-old airman, working in Air Mobility Command (AMC).

I really enjoyed [the Air Force] until the [Iraq] war started, and then I wanted out. When you're 19, you don't think [when you're] joining the military that there might be a war. I didn't anyway. I just thought of it as a job. And then, when the war started, we were loading bombs and loading food, and then downloading bodies. For me, it was just too much, at the age of 19, to handle emotionally.

I had a really hard time with it actually. I went to therapy and struggled really bad and tried to get out. But it didn't work because we were in a war, and I had a 6-year enlistment. I think it made me need my husband more, because you don't have family or anybody else to deal with the emotions. At that age, it was just too much to

---

[3] "Dependent" is a term traditionally used in the military when referring to immediate family members of a service member, typically a civilian spouse and/or child.

handle. Why were we helping people and then hurting them? Just confusion, I guess, for that young of an age.

Even when it wasn't fun, the thing that I liked the most about the military was the camaraderie, the friendship of it. I grew up a military brat, so I was used to that way of life. People moving, people from different areas, it just felt normal. But, long hours and too [many] grown-up issues when you're 19 was the hard part.

I was in a male-oriented job, which is not necessarily easy either. In our career field in the military, there are three types of women. There's the lesbians, there's the women who sleep with everybody, and then there's the bitches. And I was considered the bitch because I was married. I didn't flirt with anybody and I worked hard and believed in the rules and tried to make everybody follow the rules, so it didn't go over so good. There was the boys' club and I wasn't part of that. It made work difficult.

I was the outcast girl. They would tell the other airmen that they don't have to listen to me, but yet they would put me in charge. How am I supposed to be in charge if you're telling them they don't have to listen to me? So that was a big push to get out. I don't know…I really don't think women belong in the military.

It's such a boys' club, if you're not one of those three types…. I mean, that's pretty much the only role you can be in. If you're the hard worker, you're not going to get anywhere. Either you have to be flirting to make the guys happy or be like one of the guys. There's no room to be a secure, strong woman and not be flirting with the guys. And this is a perspective from a male-oriented job. I don't know what it's like to work medical or MPF [Military Personnel Flight][4] in the offices or something. We had a shop of 90 people and there were only 4 girls. There either needs to be more women mixed in there or a men-only career field. Because we would be out on the flight line for 12 hours a day and you would

---

[4] This function is also known as the Military Personnel Section (MPS) on some Air Force bases. Both entities provide customer support to military members regarding human resource issues.

call over the radio saying you have to go to the bathroom. And, because the guys would just go in the woods, they wouldn't let you come back. Or, if you did come back, you'd get yelled at, so it was a big mess.

After two assignments in the Air Force, Kendra decided to leave active duty. She disliked how she was treated as a woman, and found the work stressful. At a certain point, the emotional distress she experienced was too much for her, and she opted to leave the military for civilian life. While Kendra's husband remained in the Air Force, her identity shifted from active duty member to active duty spouse. She describes what this transition was like for her when they moved to New Jersey.

It was pretty stressful and lonely because my husband was on graveyard shift. So, if I was home in the apartment during the day, I had to be super quiet and I couldn't really go too many places because I had the two dogs and it was summer time and I couldn't leave them in the car. But I couldn't leave them at home because they might wake him up. But [my husband] just kept saying, "Oh, enjoy your time. You don't have to work, and you're free. You can do whatever you want." And I'm like, "I have no friends. I have no way to meet friends." When you PCS, if you're active duty, you automatically know people when you go somewhere. Because you go to your shop and you get introduced to everybody. But when you're the spouse, and this was my first PCS as a spouse, you know your husband and you don't know anybody else. I get jealous of people who have children because at least you have your kids to take with you to the store or something. So it was pretty lonely. It sucked.

It [felt] like you didn't matter anymore. After using your social security number for 6 years [to gain access to benefits], then all of a sudden your social security number doesn't count. It's *his* social security number. And then not being able to do anything on your own without him. You go and try to do something and they say,

Silent Sacrifice on the Homefront

"Well, you need your sponsor."[5] Then I'm like, "What do you mean I need my sponsor? I'm right here and he's on graveyard shift. Why can't I do it without him?" Like if you needed your ID [identification] card renewed or if you needed to get your car registered. It takes your identity away and puts it on him. I'd been the military spouse, but I'd never been the military *dependent* spouse.

Not only did Kendra's military separation change her employment status, but it also significantly changed the roles in her marriage. She was expected to take on more of the housework, and was no longer allowed to handle the military "chores" that only service members are authorized to perform. Symbolic of that change, her social security number could no longer be used for military purposes, adding to a feeling that she doesn't matter much anymore. In addition, Kendra's husband did not understand why she should complain when she was now the one with all the freedom. Where they used to be equal partners, they now seemed to be living in separate worlds.

[It was frustrating] because he didn't understand. My husband [would say], "Oh, you have all this free time and you can do whatever you want." And you're like, "Well, I want a job, that's what I want to do. Like, I'm gonna sit in the apartment all day?"

I've been on my own since I was 16 and I've had a job since I was 12, so I've always supported myself. To just sit at home and have him support me, that's not what I want for myself. He doesn't understand that because he's more than happy to support me. But that's not how I fulfill myself. I need to have a job.

Kendra is crying now...

I've taken care of myself for so long that it's scary to let someone else do it. And it's my job to do it. It's not his job to do it. If you don't have a job and he decides you're not important and leaves,

---

[5] "Sponsor" is a term used in the military to denote the person serving in the military, as opposed to "dependents" whose military benefits are sponsored by the service member.

43

then what? It's easier to take care of yourself. Always take care of yourself.

I felt lost for a while, just trying to find which direction I wanted to go. It made things between me and my husband weird, because he expected a wife now. Before, I worked more hours than he did, so he did the laundry and the dishes and the cooking. Now, the roles were reversing and I'm not a stay-at-home wife. I don't like doing that kind of stuff. And now he expected that because he did it when I was busy. Now it's my turn, but that's not what I want to do. I'd rather be out of the house and working and bringing home the money. Let someone else do that [other stuff].

It wasn't fun. There was a lot of fighting and the PCS was a lot more stressful than when we were both in [the military]. He would go to the in-processing briefings and do the claims for the broken stuff. And he would come home and I'd ask, "What did they say? Well, what about this? Did you ask this?" Normally I would do that stuff because I'm much more detail-oriented and I ask a million questions. It caused tension between us because he wasn't doing it the way I would do it and I couldn't do it anymore. That was definitely weird.

Kendra's outlook on life brightened when she learned they would be returning to Germany, back to Ramstein where she and her husband originally met while she was still on active duty. She was "really excited" about going back to a familiar place where she could regain her sense of independence.

I wanted to get a job [in Germany], but it wasn't as important as when I was in the states because I don't mind traveling around by myself, going places. I didn't need the friendship factor. This was familiar. Going to New Jersey was not familiar. For me, going to Germany was [like] coming home. So, there were no nerves or anxiousness. I was just ready to come back. I figured I'd just travel around and wait until I got a job.

[I started teaching with] the Head Start program for the Army. You teach them the basics of [how to get around] Germany, like how to ask for something to drink, or where the bathroom is. And then on Fridays, you do the field trip down to Kaiserslautern [a city near Ramstein], and give them a little tour around. I really liked it, and I'm pretty sure I was good at it.

I discovered I really like teaching. I really like to see them progressing. I have a weird obsession with Germany and I like to share the positive influence of that because a lot of people don't want to come here. And I think that it's really important that the first impression you get [is positive]. For some people, that can make or break their tour. If they know the best places to get coffee and where to buy groceries and cool places to take their kids, I think it makes it easier for a lot of people to transition. So, I basically got to teach German and talk about how cool Germany was. But, unfortunately, I stopped doing that.

It was just getting in the way of trying to travel and making plans with my husband [because the schedule was unpredictable]. Then they needed an education counselor for the Army. I enjoyed it, going in there and helping people pick colleges and figuring out their life plan. I thought that I would be making a difference for the Army guys and helping them out.

But then it just got... Okay, before I say anything bad...my Daddy's Army but the Army is definitely a different breed than the Air Force. They're very open with what they're going to tell you and their language is not appropriate for speaking to strangers sometimes. We had to call a few first sergeants[6] in and tell them, "We're afraid this guy's going to come back and hurt us." This guy came back from Iraq after a year and his dad had passed away, and the way he was screaming at us, we're like, "We're just education counselors!" But he was so angry and yelling and cussing over something. Between that and sitting in an office 8 hours a day, I would just sit there and stare at a computer. And I'm not an office person, [and there was] no interaction with people [except if] it was someone coming in to yell at you because their stuff was messed up. You get a few of the nice guys that are maybe going for their

---

[6] A first sergeant is responsible for the morale, welfare, and conduct of all the enlisted members in a military unit.

bachelor's or master's [degrees] and they are understanding and nice about it. But the bad outnumbered the good in that job. So that's when I started looking for something else to do.

[I applied to go back and do] the same thing I was doing in the military [working at the AMC passenger terminal]. I liked the job that I did in the military. It was just the military aspect at that age was not okay for me. And come to find out, I have anxiety issues, and all this stuff that I discovered now that I'm older. Maybe, had I known that when I was younger, I could have handled the situations better. So, I found that job, applied, got the interview, got the job. That was 4 months ago. I'm just kind of in that limbo not knowing when I start. Now I'm just staying home again, waiting.

I'm nervous because I'm a job person. When I got the GS⁷ job, people said, "Oh, you're set for life, a career, and you're good." And I'm like, "Oh God, I think I'm stuck." I already felt stuck just from them saying, "You're going to have a career." But I think I'm over that now, because in 3 years we'll PCS and, if I don't want to go back to a GS job, I don't have to. I can do something else.

I think because I'm such an indecisive person, and I've moved around my whole life, I'm used to [moving] every 2 or 3 years, it's got to change. So, we were in Jersey for 4 years but I had two different jobs. I changed my degree three times. It's just that I don't like it to stay the same. I'm so used to change that I don't want [one career]. I don't know, it just feels stuck. Most people are like, "Oh, I've been friends with this person for 20 years." I've been friends with my husband, but that's the longest friendship [I've ever had]. When you move every 2 or 3 years, I get to experience new people, new things, and new jobs. I like that.

I'm also excited because now that I'm older…guys [at work] can't intimidate me the way they used to, and the rank structure doesn't matter because I'm a civilian. As long as I do a good job,

---

⁷"GS" stands for General Schedule and is the federal government's system for classifying most civil service jobs. The pay scale ranges from GS-1 to GS-15.

they can't do anything to me. I think it'll be good. *Kendra begins to cry again.*

It seems like you're still kind of emotional about it.

Yeah, because I'm scared that it will be the same. It's still the military, it's still the guys' club and everything. But, it always seems like the civilians get to be different. You don't have to be in that club because you don't need their approval to progress in the ranks or get the good shift or not have to suck the poop out of the plane, you know. You just do your job, and as long as you do your job, you're good. And someone might actually see that you do a good job and you might actually get promoted; as opposed to the military, [where] you just get more work if you do a good job.

I hope it brings back that feeling of doing something, making a difference, helping people get on to the next duty station. I love when people come back from TDYs and you work in the PAX [passenger] terminal. You get to see the families reunite. That's my favorite part because you helped bring them back to their family and you get to see that. But it's also hard to watch the goodbyes. It's a reminder so you don't forget the war and the people that are down there [fighting in it]. There's still so many people that are deployed and fighting, and people don't think about it. Even military people don't think about it.

Kendra's words are positive about returning to her old shop, but her emotions are high and she admits that she is scared about returning to the same work environment. Although this part of the story is not about her marriage, it demonstrates the emotional impact a job can have on an individual, and the ripple effects it could have on life at home as well. Kendra seems to be particularly sensitive to this reality, and recognizes how her career decisions shape her as a person. She goes on to describe the impact of her employment on her sense of worth, especially because she does not have children nor want to be a "stay-at-home wife."

I think [work] gives me self-worth, because I don't have kids, and I don't like playing the stay-at-home wife role. So it kind of defines me, gives me something to get up for. Without the job, I can clean the house, but if you're home every day and there's no kids to mess it up, it's clean every time you wake up. You're like, "Okay, cleaned the house, walked the dogs, and did everything, and it's only 9:00 a.m." So it gives you something to get up for. You make friends at work and you have that camaraderie. I think that's important, especially when you're overseas, because you don't have the family or the lifelong friends. But at work, you have that. And since everybody's so transient all the time, you get closer faster. I think it's good to have those relationships.

I try to fill my time, but I don't fit in with the moms because I don't have any children. I don't have anything to input, like, "Oh, my kid did this or this." [Instead] I'm like, "I went for a walk with my dogs." So, at least with the people at work, you have work to talk about. You have that commonality, and it's easier to fit in. Right now, I feel like I don't fit [in] anywhere.

I think that's difficult for women because you're supposed to have the kid part. And if you don't have the kid part, what do you think you're going to do? You know, one mom was like, "Oh, I wish I had free time or whatever like you do!" Everybody says that, until they have the free time. If you didn't have your kids, and you were just sitting at home, what would you do? You have to feed three people every day, you have to clean up after three people. To have one person, it gets really boring.

How do you think being a military spouse has impacted you?

If I was working, and my husband was working normal jobs, I think I would get really bored, just because it would be the same. Same thing day after day and year after year. You maybe get your one vacation a year or whatever. But here, every weekend you get to travel, you get to go somewhere and see something new.

But I know it causes some strife between me and my husband, and he perceives it too. My job isn't as important as his job because I don't have to work. He makes enough money that we could live comfortably with me not working. So, I think he does get probably jealous sometimes of the guys whose wives do stay at home and just cook and clean and be that wife and be content with that.

I would love it if *he* stayed at home, and cooked and cleaned and did everything. But I wouldn't expect that.

Kendra ends her story with this contrast between what her husband expects and what she wishes her husband would want for her. She understands the desire to have someone take care of the household since she would love to have someone do this for her, but also seems a bit sad that her husband may not understand her desire to do more. Just as she doesn't expect him to be the primary caretaker at home, she doesn't believe he should expect this of her either. Now that she is embarking on full-time federal employment, they will be challenged with the task of reconciling their disparate expectations of each other.

Nicole

"I think the biggest thing is that, either way, my husband supported me."

Nicole has been an investigator with the Department of Defense for the past 13 years. She was fortunate enough to turn her husband's PCS relocations into career advancement opportunities for herself. When he received orders to Alaska, Nicole made a successful pitch to her superiors about opening a branch at that location. Building on that experience, she was then promoted into a position at his next assignment in Monterey, California. At the time of our interview, she is on leave without pay because her agency did not have a position available in Germany when they moved there. Now she is reflecting on her career so far and her options for the future. She also describes what it was like for her to move up the ranks in her agency as a working mother, and how critical the support of her husband has been.

I was an investigator with the federal government, and I'd already been a federal employee for almost 5 years when [my husband and I] met. I loved it and enjoyed it. I was really thankful to have the job and my husband was very supportive. When we got our orders to go to Alaska, I was a little apprehensive because right away I knew we didn't have a field office in Alaska. So I started thinking, "Okay, am I going to have a job?"

But it turned out to be a really great career experience and professional growth for me. I went to our agency and said, "Hey, look. We're moving up there. I know you guys send TDY support." I did a points paper explaining and justifying why we needed a field office up there. And with management support, they allowed that. We moved up there and I opened up the field office. I felt like, "Okay, great, I'm making a difference." I was really contributing to the overall mission DoD wide because of the nature of what we do. And it was great. I loved it.

While Nicole recognizes her good fortune during their first two assignments, she says being a career-oriented military spouse still has its challenges. Many of those sacrifices fell on her shoulders.

I will say that, being a spouse, you make a lot of sacrifices. I feel that you make a lot of sacrifices because my husband didn't have a lot of flexibility with his job [in Alaska]. Both our sons were born up there, and he was definitely able to help with dropping off and picking up at daycare. But I realized how much his career came first because he didn't have the flexibility being active duty to say, "Here are my work hours." The Air Force bottom line is you work when they need you to work, based on mission requirements. And I totally understand that. But thank goodness that I had the flexibility I did. So the thought went through my mind, "What if we were someplace else and I wasn't able to take off?" That would be another challenge that we would have to address just because he didn't have the flexibility. And he wasn't in a position to say, "Well, I'm just not going to go to work." I mean, as a squadron commander, you just can't do that.

For me, it's a tough reality to swallow. It really is, because that means his job is more important than mine. And I know that he doesn't feel that way, but the reality is, he's the one that's in the Air Force. He's the one that's making a career out of it. And we even talked about [if] I wanted him to get out, then I would be the breadwinner, and he would find a job elsewhere. But I said, "No, I'm comfortable with the way things are. I don't want to be the sole breadwinner." I'm independent, driven, and ambitious, but at the same time, I wasn't ready to say, "Okay, yes. Let's focus on my career first and then you can get a job that's based around my career." I'm also very old fashioned and like to let the man make the money.

Nicole's comments here are interesting in that they reflect some mixed feelings about her career. Although she is frustrated by the reality that her husband's career is primary as long as he is in the military, she does not accept her husband's offer to get out and allow her career to take the lead. She appreciates her husband's willingness to support her career

51

completely, but still prefers not to become the primary breadwinner. While she calls herself "old fashioned," Nicole also sticks by her decision to be a working mother, even when she was haunted by doubts about her choices.

[When my kids were born] I did not take a break, with the exception of my 3 months' maternity leave. And I have to tell you, it was very, very emotional [when I returned to work]. With my oldest, I probably cried the first month. I had 12 weeks with him and I thought, "I don't know if I want to go back to work." I really surprised myself, because I thought for sure I'd want to go back to work. But I cried that first month dropping him off and picking him up thinking, "Man, I don't know that this is the right decision."

But then I realized that I wasn't really ready to give up my job. And seeing him thrive in that daycare setting, I didn't feel like I was missing out on any parts of his life. I didn't work really long hours and I was nursing him, so every day for lunch I went and nursed him. Also, my job was really great with me because I told them I don't want to travel this first year. They were very accommodating. So that made it hard, too, that professional commitment and pride. And I thought, "Okay, they're willing to work with me so I don't want to just quit." And that's what I felt like I'd be doing is just quitting on my job and my career. And I felt like I had worked hard to get to where I was. I was really enjoying it. So weighing all of that, I felt okay. I'm going to move forward and this is going to be fine, and I did. And it was. But it was tough. I tried to go part time, actually, but they said, "No."

I felt almost guilty putting my work first. And then some of the spouses in the spouses' group were openly against women working outside of the home. So there was, "Well, I wouldn't leave my son or daughter in daycare." And that's what I had to hear. I thought, "God, am I a bad mother for choosing work over my son or for putting him in a daycare?" But no, I wasn't. It was the right decision. It was a good decision. And I'm happy about that. In hindsight, I wouldn't have done it any differently at all. And I don't feel any less close to him because of that time. I feel like I'm a better mother because I have a professional outlet. I have something that's mine. Emotionally, professionally, I feel very fulfilled. And I think having that outlet helps me to be a better mother.

Despite how some other spouses judged her, Nicole came away from her experience feeling satisfied that working made her a better mother. Being able to play that role, however, required lots of practical support from her husband. Nicole describes her challenges to juggle home and work life as she continues to advance within her agency and take on more responsibility. Her husband's willingness to become the primary parent was critical to her success in this regard.

Now I went from being career professional to being career professional and a wife, then being career professional, wife, and mom. And really it's mom, wife, career professional – in that order. So I'd like to say I put my husband first, but I think he and I both put our children first. And, emotionally, it was at times very challenging to fill all of those roles. Sometimes I was just drained from work or travel, or the boys maybe had a tough day. And then my husband came home and wanted attention as well, and I'm thinking, "I'm just so tired. I really just have no energy left to talk. I just want to go to bed."

I think the biggest thing is that, either way, my husband supported me. He said, "If you don't want to go to work anymore and you want to be a stay-at-home mom, you go ahead." But then, at the same time, he said, "You really want to think about that because knowing the way I know you, you may regret not working." So knowing I had the option to stay at home or not was wonderful. At the same time, he made an effort to get away from work when he could to make dinner or help with the housework. He's always been very good at that. So that's been great. And then the times when I went TDY, he was there taking care of the kids and trying to arrange his schedule so that he could do the drop off and the pick up, and just doing everything for the couple of days that I was gone. I don't take that for granted. So that was another example of how he was supportive.

Then my agency asked, "Would you mind stepping up and being the Acting Field Office Chief just for a temporary period?"

Not that I was afraid of the challenge, but there was a 1½-hour drive [to the field office]. So I thought, "Okay, I'll bite the bullet and do this, because who knows where we're going to move to next." I thought this would be another great opportunity.

I felt very confident [that] I could do the job. But, logistically, it didn't work. I didn't want to have to do that commute every single day. I just didn't want to do it. I was worn out. I was pretty exhausted physically and emotionally and not feeling good about myself. I had gained weight, sitting in the car, eating whatever. I wasn't eating healthy. And then I had a lot of time away from my kids. Sometimes I didn't get home until 7:30 at night. My kids were already going to bed, if not already in bed. And I hadn't seen them in the morning because I was leaving the house at 5:00 to miss traffic. So I said, "No, I can't do it anymore."

During that time, my husband did everything. I would not have been able to do the job for even the 4 months I did, had it not been for his love and support. He was the one that picked up and dropped off the kids, cooked dinner, cleaned the house. He did all of that. And that was because, at the time, he really had an eight-to-five job. So, I would not have been able to do that without his support.

[Then we found out we were going to Germany] and I wanted to go overseas. I really did. And, quite truthfully, I was so burned out from my job, it was an easy out for me. I didn't have to make the choice, because there's no overseas office. I wanted a break. I needed a break. I said, "Yay! Let's go."

As Nicole describes it, moving to Germany was a welcome change. She was able to step off the fast track she had been on at work and take a break. Since her agency had no office in Germany, she was able to take a year off without pay while maintaining her status within the federal system. Now she is pondering what is next for her, how she feels about staying out of the workforce, and how important advancement may be to her.

Getting back to the emotional side, I think I miss that professional fulfillment. I really do. I really miss working with great people. I really miss contributing to a mission. I really miss the challenges and the rewards. And then I have nearly 13 years vested with the government. So, my professional goal at this state would be to get to 20 [years of service]. I'm on leave without pay, and I do want to continue working for the federal government. Ideally, I'd like to stay with my agency. But if that doesn't come to fruition, I'd better start applying now because the process can take a little while. In July, my leave without pay is up.

Overall, it's been great and it's been a much-needed break, absolutely. I'm very thankful. I'm very thankful that I didn't have to work, and that my agency didn't call me and say, "Can you work now?"

Now I'm missing work, now that I feel like we've settled into a routine, and I know the boys are going to be in school next year every day. So now I'm focusing more on my job again. And I'm starting to worry about what I am going to do. So that's kind of where I am now. My hope is that I can stay with the federal government and maintain my grade, even a GS-11 or GS-12 would be fine. *Nicole was previously working as a GS-13 pay grade.*

My hope is that I can maintain that and work to get my 20 years in. And based on where we are at that point in our life, and how the boys are doing especially, then I'll determine whether or not I want to keep working or not. So that's what my hope is, to have a fulfilling job where I can maintain my pay grade, while also being a great mom and making sure that the boys are developmentally and academically where they need to be in their life, and are having the opportunities I had when I was that age.

Every day is just kind of an emotional roller coaster because some days I thank God I'm not working. I really love this break. I really love all my time. I love being able to have lunch with my girlfriends and go to the gym and just be carefree. It's like, "Woo-hoo!" I've never had this before. But then other days I'm like, "I don't want to go to lunch. I'm tired of the gym. I can work out on the weekends. I want to work." So it's been emotional that way. And my husband continues to be supportive, saying, "Well, if you want to go back to work, great. But, if you don't, that's fine, too."

55

At the same time, he's like, "You're not going to apply for a GS-9, are you? You're a GS-13. You don't need to go back."

To have a career, not just a job, is something that's very challenging as a military spouse. There's what you would like, and then there's what the reality is and what you can get. And a lot of times those two things don't jive. So, I feel like I'm stuck settling. I'm stuck settling for what's available versus what I really want.

It's a tough reality, but it's certainly one that I expected. When we met and when we married, I knew that was going to happen. I really did. But knowing it and experiencing it are two different things. Knowing what I did back then, I would still do it all over again. It's worth the sacrifice. It really is. It sucks some days, for lack of a better term, but overall, I wouldn't have it any other way. I feel like my husband will finish at 20 [years] and then, at that point in time, I would like to go to a place where my career can soar. And I know he would be supportive of that. So, you know what? If I have to put my career on hold right now, I will. Now that won't stop me from trying to move forward. But if it doesn't work out, then it just doesn't work out. It's not meant to be and that's just the way it is.

At the end of our interview, Nicole remains unsettled about her future but confident that it will work out. Although she is unsure if she will be able to maintain her current pay grade within the federal system, she feels fortunate that her husband will support her regardless. Her preference is to continue advancing her career; however, she is aware that she may be at a temporary, or even permanent, plateau for her within the federal system. Having the freedom to explore all options, including jobs at a lower pay grade or taking a break from employment, gives her the reassurance that she can choose the best alternative for her. Knowing her husband's support is unwavering is a constant she can count on, despite any other setbacks she may encounter along the way.

Felice

"This is not just marrying someone who has a job. This is marrying the military. And this is a very hard thing."

Felice is a newlywed, trying to make sense of her two new marriages: one to her husband and one to the military. She is struggling to find a way to stay positive and make her own career a priority. Felice is currently unemployed after working several years in the Human Resources (HR) field. During our interview, Felice talks about the importance of working as a source of self-worth, and repeatedly reflects on the connection between her employment and how she feels about her marriage. She is trying to reconcile the lessons she learned from her own mother about the importance of a career while wanting to accommodate the needs of her new life as a military spouse. Felice begins our interview reflecting back on her perspective on work and the lessons of her childhood.

I've always been the type of person who gets my self-worth or self-fulfillment from achievements. I grew up in a two-parent household where both my parents worked. My mother was a nurse and she ran a hospice. She was the director of a hospice. And my dad worked at a national laboratory, and he did all the budgets – very highly educated people, very busy. They had five kids and they both had to work. My mother loved her job, absolutely loved her job. And then she came home and raised her five children. And that was something that was instilled in me from such an early age. I'm the youngest of five children, and when I was born, she went back to work. My whole childhood, I always saw my mother working. So worthiness for me comes into play because I saw that she did everything, and she loved her job. And there were times that my dad would say [to her], "Well, you know, you don't have to work if you don't want to." And she would look at him like he was crazy. "I have to work because this makes me feel good about myself."

So having that as a mentor… Worthiness to me is based on achievement. My mother achieved a lot and still had the family and still had all of that. So I felt like I should always work because if she could do it, then I could too. And always be the best of the best of the best because I felt like that's when you get recognition. Being in such a large family, you get recognition when you stand out.

Felice sounds firm in her convictions when she describes the family she came from and the values she learned about the importance of work. Long ago, she came to the conclusion that work is the source of achievement, recognition, and, therefore, self-worth. Now that she is unemployed, she seems to lack not only the recognition she used to enjoy, but also her sense of conviction about her purpose.

I've always been on a path of high outward achievement, but now I've had the time to step back, because I'm not working, and say, "What do I *really* want?" And to be honest with you, I don't know.

I was very nervous from the work perspective [when I got married], but I decided in my head that it's okay. You're going to marry this person. You are not going to pass this up [when] you don't know what's next for you in terms of work. So I thought, "Okay, maybe I'll come [to Germany] and get a master's degree so at least I'm furthering myself or doing something. Or maybe it will be amazing. I'll find a job and all of that." But until I'm living it, until I'm in the situation, you can try to warn me and talk to me about it a hundred times. My husband does that very well. Here's every single situation that could ever happen. And, of course, I was listening to him at the time – but until I'm living it on a daily basis, I couldn't always make those connections.

Although Felice was aware that military life would present challenges to her career, she admits that she did not fully appreciate how profound those impacts would be until she actually experienced them. From an analytic perspective, she could rationalize what the anticipated consequences would be of moving around with the military. Now that she is living that experience, however, her emotions rule the day and have convinced her that she may have underestimated the change she was about to make.

The biggest thing that is really difficult about being here [in Europe] is that it's the double-edged sword of time to travel and not work, versus what's going to be on that resume when I go back to the states next April and it has nothing on it. I come from HR, I come from recruiting, and if I saw that resume I would put it to the side. Realistically, I'm not going to put down that I'm a military spouse or that I moved based on being a military spouse. As a recruiter, [you know] that person is leaving in 3 to 5 years.

This is not just marrying someone who has a job. This is marrying the military. And this is a very hard thing. In my opinion, it is two marriages because there is something that dictates where you are going to live. What if that area of the country doesn't even do what you do?

Felice delivers her bottom line assessment that her struggle is based on the reality that she is trying to adjust to two marriages, not just one. Perhaps she anticipated the transition to marrying her husband but did not fully appreciate how much the military would influence their marriage, or how she would feel about her new life. Now she toggles back to the question of job searching and what she should do with her time in Germany. For her, this is a sticky question that she deems critical to her feelings of self-worth as well as feelings about her marriage. Central to this question is whether or not she should consider taking a low-wage job for which she is overqualified.

If the job doesn't pay what you were making, that's another difficult scenario as well. What's my self-worth if I'm making $8 an hour when I was making $55,000 a year? I went for an interview [when we got here] and I was very overqualified for the job. It was a front desk position, really not handling a lot. The position paid $7.50 [an hour] but they said they would give me $8 an hour. There was going to be no time off for the first 90 days, just like any normal job. They knew I was overqualified. I mean, I had done more than what the director of the program was doing at the time. And I kind of felt uncomfortable because I didn't want her to feel like, "Who's this person who knows more than I do?" So I really tried to dumb myself down. Even though it showed I'd done all this stuff on my resume. And I just [said], "I am willing to take an entry-level position." That was a question they asked me. So I went for the interview.

I felt pretty good, but I brought it home to my husband as well. This was the first time I've ever asked someone else's opinion on my work stuff, which felt uncomfortable, but I said, "Now we're a team. So I guess this is a decision we both make, you know?" And he was like, "I just don't know how you can feel good about that. I mean, you were making this amount. Now you're going to make $8 an hour, and we're going to lose all our flexibility. You're not going to be able to travel. What if you don't have the same days off as I do?" And I bought into it. I said, "You're right. We're here to travel. This is our time." We just got married, all of that. So I bought into that, and I was okay with that. And then I got the call for the second interview. And I know I would have gotten the job, but I didn't accept the second interview.

And then as the months have gone on, of course, my husband and I travel. Of course, we do that. We're doing 3-day weekends, that type of thing. My husband moved from a position where he was working in one area and then he was actually promoted to be an exec [executive officer] to a commander. So now he's much busier. Now he doesn't get home until 7:00 or 8:00 at night. Now he's not even home. And here I am holding off, not getting a job, regretting not going for that second interview, and if I was offered the job, not taking it. Were the 10 days of travel that we've done in the last 5 months worth me not working?

This example of the missed job opportunity weighs heavily on Felice. Although she is dismissive about the value of the job, she is also focused on what the job represented for her. She could have found something to do with her day where she could have been recognized for her accomplishments. Instead, she agreed with her husband to forego the job and maintain her flexibility to be available to him. Felice acknowledges how vulnerable this decision made her feel, allowing someone else, for the first time, to have input into her employment decisions. Although they may have made a rational decision for the right reasons, on an emotional level, Felice is resentful. Ironically, by making a choice to preserve their flexibility to travel and enjoy Europe, Felice is left feeling restricted in her ability to pursue something meaningful for herself. Our interview continues with some reflections about the implications for her marriage.

It's hard. There's resentment toward my husband that isn't his fault. This is his job. This is what he's doing. But then I'm watching Dr. Phil and I'm saying to him, "I already saw that this morning." And he's like, "Must be nice to watch TV." So then you have this power struggle of saying, "But I listened to your advice. And you decided with me that it wasn't a good idea to take a job because we would lose our flexibility. But now I don't know when you're coming home from work. And I'm alone all day, and yes I can go have lunch with people, and live this weird lifestyle." I'm not putting down anybody by saying this, but I'm like the lady who lunches. You know? I don't have any responsibilities. I don't have anything to do. I don't know when my husband is coming home from work, so sometimes dinner is made, sometimes it's not. I get to it when I get to it. I clean our house, but I don't get gratification out of cleaning my house. That doesn't make me feel like I'm giving to my relationship. Also the factor of money, none of this money is mine anymore, in my head. This isn't money I brought to our marriage. And that's really difficult. I want to buy something, and before, when I was single and working, I just bought it.

It's our money, and my husband doesn't feel this way, but I feel that I have to be telling him what I buy. And I don't like that. I have so much guilt about it. Where really he'd be like, "Honey, I don't care. That's fine." But you know the $100 pair of Coach shoes I bought? Do I really need those? And why do I feel so guilty for not telling him I bought them? He sees the Discover [credit card] bill. It's not like the guy doesn't know I buy stuff, but I have this guilt because I'm not contributing. I've never been in that space where I didn't support myself and it's really hard on the esteem for me.

Like I said, I base things on achievements. Cleaning my house is not an achievement.

Felice seems to be in a downward spiral now, where the lack of a job has caused her to question just about everything. Without a purpose to her day and a way of demonstrating achievement, she is at loose ends. She feels guilty for not contributing, and frustrated that her husband doesn't seem to understand her feelings. Felice goes on to describe how scared and helpless she feels about her future.

I'm not saying there aren't things for me to be doing. I just kind of feel scared, which I've never felt before. [I'm scared that] I'm not going to be awesome at [what I do], or that it's not going to work out, or I'm going to fall in love with something and as soon as I get in a rhythm and feel good, we're going to get orders and go somewhere else. And it's also building connections with other women as well. You build these connections and then, "See you later." So how much do you really give of yourself? How much do you really invest in relationships with other people? And how do you not complain? My husband has taken an oath to do this. This is a very honoring position, what he's decided to do with his life. And here I am, spending my 8 hours a day complaining about it. I chose this. I really own my choices, and I've been that person where I commit to something full force. But like I said, I have controlled everything in my life. Now I literally feel like I have no control.

I'm compensating for not being busy by buying things. [My husband] had told me this a while ago. Before we were married, he's like, "Yeah, some of the guys come to work and they complain about how their wives just spend all this money." And I understand why now. They have nothing to do. And they need to be validated. So when they see something they want, or it's a trip to the BX [Base Exchange], it's somewhere to go. I thought, "God, that's so lame." Now I'm that person.

And I think what's difficult, too, is that I am newly married. So this is a formative time for my relationship and here I am in shock mode. Oh, my gosh, this is my life and how will I ever have a job?

How will I ever do this when everything right now is based on him? So it's coming together as a couple, but it's also like I said: the two marriages. Realizing this thing is the military, that's the marriage.

I'll ask my husband how his day is, and I know he appreciates that. But when he asks me about my day, I don't want to talk about it, because I'm like, "Well, I didn't do anything today. I sat on the couch all day. God, I'm totally worthless."

My self-worth comes from people feeling like I did a good job. Sometimes I'll say to my husband, "I washed the car and I mowed the lawn today." And he'll say, "Oh, great, whatever." No, I need the recognition for doing that. He's like, "Sweetheart, this is life. Sometimes you got to mow the lawn and sometimes you got to wash the car." But I'm not working. I need recognition for something. If our house looks clean, I need you to make a big deal out of it. I was never like this before. I seek gratification because I'm not going to get it from anything else.

Self-worth is a recurring theme for Felice, and she is quick to judge herself for not accomplishing more. She also feels the need for more recognition from her husband since there are no other sources of achievement in her life. As she piles on numerous reasons for feeling frustrated, she admits that she is still in "shock mode." Still only a few months into her marriage, she is just beginning to make sense of the conflicting emotions she is feeling. One feeling she is grappling with is a lack of confidence or a sense of being defeated.

I hope I can get back in the workforce and be where I was at because I don't even feel confident to be where I was at. I don't feel confident to ask for $55,000 knowing I've been out of the workforce for a year. I don't feel confident because, from my perspective as a recruiter, I have a massive gap on my resume. So, I hope I find a job. Or maybe I'll just go back [to school] so I can avoid putting that resume together to try to get a job.

I decided I was going to get a master's while I'm here. And I go in to talk to [the Education Office] about it, and I tell the lady, "Here's my $40 application fee." And she says, "Well, when's the

DEROS[8] date? When do you leave?" And here's where I get defeated. She says, "You can't do the program. You have to complete the master's while you're here [and there isn't enough time]. It's only an overseas program for counseling. Sorry, that's the policy." So how are you really helping me, you know? You're totally defeating me. Now I'm not going to get a master's while I'm here. A door is closed, and it makes me want to give up.

It's this whole new life that I don't control a lot of, in my perspective. And my thought pattern is that I just need to take the bull by the horns and just make it happen for myself. But when I try to do that, like I said, I get this defeated attitude. I don't know where that's coming from.

I feel like I'm the only one who can make it happen for myself. It's not my husband's responsibility to make it happen for me. It is my responsibility to make my own happiness that I can share with him. I told my husband I don't think we're going to have kids for 5 years. What do I have to bring to the table? I don't have a job. I don't know what I'm doing. I want my children to be proud of me. I want to have something so when they do go to school, I have my own thing going on. I need to figure that out. I need to go to nursing school, if that's what I'm going to do, before I have a child.

I remember when I first came here and all the women I met had children. Either their husbands were enlisted or they were officers, but they immediately had children when they got in. And I said, "Oh, I feel bad for these ladies. All they've known is kids." But then that thought came into my mind the other day. Well, maybe I'll have a baby. No, you don't have a baby to chart the course because you don't know where the course is going. You have a baby because you're ready to have a baby. But I can kind of see why some people made those choices. So, of course, I'm not going to bring another life here. But then I'm thinking to myself, "Well, what else am I doing?" And that's kind of the crazy soliloquy that's going on in

---

[8] DEROS stands for Date Eligible for Return from Overseas and refers to the anticipated end date of an overseas assignment.

my head, because I've got a lot of time on my hands to overthink and overanalyze every single thing. And then my husband will come home and say, "God, you look so stressed out." That's because I've been thinking about crazy things for the last 8 hours for this entire week, every single day.

Or I feel obligated to get up in the morning with my husband when he has PT [physical training]. I'll get up at 6:30 in the morning because, when we first got here, I was sleeping in until noon. Then he would come home and be like, "Oh, my God, why is your hair wet?" Because I basically just took a shower 15 minutes before you came home. I didn't do anything today. Now I try to get up and I try to stay up, [even if] I don't have a plan today. So it's just weird. I've never been this way. I've never been like, "Oh, my God, how am I going to fill the day?" If I don't have anything, he knows I'm on the couch all day. That's not healthy for me. That's not mentally healthy. I don't have anything, so I'm kicking my fins trying to stay above water, because I feel like there is no control.

I've expressed this to my husband too. I know I felt more confident and had more self-worth when I had a job. So I don't have a job; hence, I feel this way. It also has other factors too. It's not just being a military spouse. It's being a new spouse. It's all of those things.

Felice continues to believe that her confidence and self-worth are dependent on having a job. Wrapped in that belief is her desire for a marriage that will allow her career to flourish. Just as she is willing to support her husband's career goals, more than anything, she wants a marriage that will be supportive of her own goals. She is fearful that anything less will be damaging to their relationship.

I'm [not] just going to be living for my husband. That's not who I am. I can't just take a backseat on my own life because his job dictates these parameters or whatever. And at the same time, I want to be a good spouse and I want to be supportive of the person who is supporting us financially. It must be hard to be the one who goes to work every day. I try to look at it from his perspective too. I'm sure there are days he doesn't want to go to work.

My hope is that we can come to an understanding that I'm going to be working and that I'm going to need to have something of my own. That's obviously going to affect our relationship if I don't have something of my own. It already affects our relationship now. Military spouses are the reason people stay in the military. We are a retention piece. So if we are not happy, we make the military member unhappy and maybe they'll get out earlier. I don't want that for my husband. I want him to have the most amazing career. I want him to do everything he possibly can. I do want everything that he wants for his career. I want him to want that same thing for me, though. And I don't know how that's going to work.

Throughout this interview, Felice does not sugarcoat her feelings or try to be positive when that is not how she feels. Her complaints are many, from loss of self-worth to lack of understanding from her husband. Some may read this story and dismiss Felice as overly negative. However, it is important to understand that she may be using this interview as a way to honestly make sense of her conflicting emotions. By talking out loud, she is testing her beliefs, her emotions, and perhaps a way forward for herself. While it may sound like venting, she may be taking the first step toward finding a healthy way of adjusting to her new life. That first step is laying all her thoughts and emotions out on the table and looking at them honestly, regardless of how daunting they may be. This interview is a safe place for her to do just that.

Felice's unflinching negativity also represents a refreshingly raw look at feelings many military spouses experience but often attempt to hide from others. Although our military culture encourages us to be resilient and positive in the face of adversity, we have all felt defeated at times, just like Felice. Particularly in her reflections about marriage, Felice's story is an important reminder about the pull of two marriages – one to a person and one to the military as an institution. Navigating life plans and career goals with another person can be challenging enough without adding a third partner to the mix. Felice illustrates that sometimes those two forces can be so intertwined that it is difficult or even impossible to separate one's feelings about the person from one's feelings about the institution. For the real marriage to be healthy, both partners must be willing to conquer military life together with explicit agreements about managing careers, household, and family.

Lessons on Marriage

What do the stories in this chapter tell us about marriage? I hope you, as the reader, have found pieces of each story that resonate with your experience. Perhaps some of these women have raised issues you have grappled with in your own marriage. As portraits of unique individual lives, these stories can't be reduced to a few simple lessons that will solve all challenges. I do want to highlight a few themes, however, that struck me as particularly useful insights for other military spouses:

1. **Roles in a marriage are sticky.** I remember learning about the concept of "stickiness" in my first college economics class. This general rule of economics states that once the price for a product is established, it can be difficult to change that price. In other words, the price is sticky or resistant to change; consumers and suppliers both become accustomed to a general price point that becomes the norm. This concept also applies to agreements made within a marriage. Once roles are established, they are hard to change, especially if one or both parties is particularly attached to the status quo. Brenda demonstrates the harsh reality of this dynamic when she tries to go back to work but can't seem to change her role as sole caretaker at home. Brenda's husband has no incentive to take on household tasks because he is comfortable in his role of being singularly focused on his job outside the home. Although Brenda complains about her situation, she also seems reluctant to work out a compromise with her husband. How could they begin to share household roles? What tasks could they outsource by paying someone to help them (e.g., cleaning or childcare)?

    Marriage does require negotiation and compromise, which can be particularly hard when roles have been set for some time. *Yet, doing the hard work to reach a compromise that both parties can live with is essential, not only for a happy marriage but also for a sustainable career.*

2. **Marriages evolve as individuals grow and change.** While roles in a marriage can be intractable, marriages can and do evolve. Serena and Lisa both demonstrate this reality in their stories. Serena starts off her marriage thinking that working is a necessary way for her to maintain her independence, but then realizes she can contribute in other ways as an equal partner. Discovering this new perspective on marriage gives her the freedom to relax a bit into her role and worry less about figuring out a career right away. Similarly, Lisa and her husband start out their marriage with the idea that she will be the primary breadwinner when he retires from the military, but this plan fades away over time as Lisa's flying career does not materialize in the way she had hoped. She does not think of this as a failure, but instead accepts this as a natural result of life turning out a bit differently than they had anticipated. Both Serena and Lisa are able to adapt to their situations by reframing the expectations of their marriage to fit the realities of their lives without building up bitterness or resentment.

3. **Marriage isn't always fair.** One of the most memorable parts of Lisa's interview for me is the moment when she discusses her husband's unwillingness to live apart during the week so she can keep her job. Although she is happy with the job and finds the arrangement reasonable, her husband is adamant that living apart during the week is not acceptable. Each time I read this part of the transcript I find myself wondering how he can be so inflexible when his job requires year-long deployments. My reaction is always, "That's not fair!" But healthy marriages are not based on games of accounting and keeping track of who has given

69

more. Marriage isn't always "fair" in that sense and Lisa understands this. She does not try to change his mind based on fairness, but acknowledges that the geographic separation has taken a toll on her marriage, something that she wants to remedy. She is more concerned about preserving her marriage as a unit than receiving fair treatment as an individual.

In many ways, this is a lesson for all military spouses. By the very nature of our military life, our marriages will never be fair. There will always be aspects of our lives outside our control (moves, deployments, last-minute work demands), and expecting fairness just isn't realistic. Our careers will be impacted in some way, whether we like it or not. We can and should be resilient and tenacious in creating the lives we desire, but fairness will never be part of the equation. If we expect that from our marriages, we are destined for disappointment.

4. **The need for independence has to be balanced by a willingness to be vulnerable.** Several of the women in this chapter mention the importance of being independent, but Kendra is the most honest by sharing her fears about being dependent. If one becomes too dependent on her spouse, and he decides to leave her, then what is she left with? For Kendra, the prospect of being financially dependent on someone else feels too risky. Serena shares similar thoughts, but arrives at a different conclusion. She is reluctant at first to let someone else take care of her, but then decides she needs to take that risk in order for her marriage to work. She decides that she can contribute to her marriage in ways beyond household income. This lesson is a fine balance. The need for emotional and financial independence is real, and military spouses (like all spouses) need to be prepared to survive if their marriage doesn't last. At the same time,

however, marriage requires vulnerability. To be in true partnership means taking enough risk to share your fears and being open to new ways of thinking and being. The trick is finding where your comfort zone is and striking the right balance between independence and vulnerability.

5. **Actions matter more than words.** Nicole's story is a perfect example of true partnership in a marriage. Not only does her husband say that he supports her career efforts, but he backs up these words with real actions. He becomes the primary caretaker when Nicole's job becomes the more demanding one. He is even willing to leave the military and let her career take the lead. His actions speak volumes and show Nicole that she has absolute support in her career aspirations. Nicole's story is a sharp contrast to Brenda's situation where neither she nor her husband seem to be able to envision a way for him to engage in household responsibilities.

   Brenda claims her husband has an "excuse job" that gets him out of such roles, which is a dynamic that occurs in many military marriages. We (the military spouse) can't possibly expect him (the service member) to stay home with a sick child, be the one to drive the carpool, or pick up the groceries after work when he has such a demanding job. But, why not? Sometimes we are a little too quick to let them off the hook and we take on too much as a result. One reason stems from ingrained gender stereotypes that influence all of us.

   For example, I know one military couple where the wife is the service member and the husband is a stay-at-home dad. Although she works a full duty day, she still does all the grocery shopping, cooks every night, and does all the laundry. Although only one example, this anecdote

71

demonstrates the power of gender roles and how much we get sucked into those norms. How strange would it sound if a female military spouse stayed home all day and did not do any of the household tasks, while the male service member worked all day and did all of the housework? The bottom line is, don't let the excuse job take on a life of its own. Service members, male or female, can and should share the load at home to some degree and back up their words with real actions.

6. **Military spouses have to juggle two marriages.** Felice is not the first person to claim that military spouses are married to the military. It's a long-standing metaphor that has some truth to it. Felice feels burdened by her adjustment as a newlywed, not only to her husband but also to military life. She expected to go through the normal transition that newly married couples experience – learning each other's habits and establishing the norms for their life together – but didn't fully anticipate how much her marriage would be impacted by their military lifestyle. As she sorts out her career options, Felice is still a bit dumbfounded by this reality. How will she juggle not just one marriage, but two? At one time or another, most military spouses are faced with this challenge. What sort of standing will the military have in your relationship, and how will you and your partner navigate the demands imposed by military life? Will you embrace this third partner, struggle to keep it at bay, or leave it behind entirely?

Questions for Reflection

Now that you've read the stories in this chapter, this may be a good opportunity for you to reflect on your own marriage and consider how well your marriage fits with the other parts of your life, including your career plans. I recommend that you read through the following questions and pick one or two that resonate with you. Take those questions that you want to explore further and write down your answers in a private journal. Or you may want to discuss them together with your spouse and compare your answers. There are no perfect marriages, and no right answers, but these questions may help you identify where you want to make a few adjustments and improve how this "M" of marriage fits in with the rest of your life.

1. Does your spouse understand what your current career goals are? Is this something you feel comfortable talking about together?
2. How well does your spouse support your career goals through words and actions? What more do you need from him/her?
3. Are you happy with the way you currently share household responsibilities with your spouse? How would you change your roles if you could?
4. What is one thing you want your spouse to know about how you feel that you haven't told him/her?
5. In what ways does the "excuse job" impact your marriage?
6. How do you feel about having the military as a second marriage?
7. How well do you balance independence versus vulnerability in your marriage? Would you do anything differently to strike a better balance?
8. What resentments about unfairness do you need to let go of?

Chapter 3 – Motherhood

Parenting is often touted as the classic work-family conflict for American workers, and is hardly a challenge specific to military spouses. For many of these military spouses, however, motherhood is often the last straw for a career already faltering or proving difficult to maintain. And although male spouses also increasingly feel the pull of parenting roles, the weight of this problem still falls primarily on female military spouses, who make up 92% of our spouse population (Department of Defense, 2016). In a recent survey, 40% of male military spouse respondents claimed that childcare issues have not impacted their careers, while only 17% of female military spouse respondents made the same claim (Blue Star Families, 2017). When it comes to parenting and childcare concerns, gender norms play a big role. We live in a society at large and a military community that still value a traditional mothering role: the mother who is the go-to parent for most things, and a mother that is ever-present, all-knowing, and the ultimate caretaker. Reconciling that ideal with the realities of a career can be a tall, if not impossible, task.

The stories in this chapter offer a range of ways in which real-life women have addressed their mothering role. Some fully embrace the traditional ideal of a stay-at-home mom and have opted for that path despite the personal pain they may feel as a result of sacrificing career. Others have found that maintaining a career focus has helped them feel like better mothers, with more of themselves to offer their children.

Grace is a stay-at-home mom who feels that living overseas for multiple assignments has given her the freedom to choose to stay home. With a successful career in business before moving overseas, she believes she would have felt pressured to continue her career if she had become a mother while living in the United States where working would have been a more viable option. She feels good about the years she has stayed home, but also wants to be a role model for her girls and says that going back to work in some form would be a positive thing.

Andrea has also taken a break in her career since her first child experienced serious health problems. She had planned to go back to work, but decided being home with her daughter was more important. Although it was difficult at first to come to terms with this decision, she says she is happy now because she knows she is "not failing." She believes she is serving an important role in her children's development, which is rewarding to her, although she looks forward to resuming her career in a few years.

Tanya has mixed feelings about her decision to stay home with her two toddlers. Although she says these have been the worst years of her life, she is also glad she has been there to care for her children and not miss the important moments. She believes being home with them is the right thing, but also says she would take a job if the right one came along. She longs to pursue an administrative career and have a break from the routine chores at home.

Katie speaks with passion about her former career as an athletic trainer, and the excitement she feels about this role is palpable. On an intellectual level, she rationalizes that her role as a mother is more important and it is a sacrifice she is willing to make in order to fill the need created by her husband's unpredictable schedule. Although she wouldn't change the decisions she has made, she admits that the pain she's felt from giving up a part of herself has been real.

Isabelle was a single mom for several years before marrying her current husband. Because she previously had to work as the sole breadwinner, she feels relieved that she can now count on a partner. Having always dreamed of the opportunity to stay home with her daughter, she stopped working for a short time, until she realized "the grass is not always greener on the other side." She discovered that she missed the structure and purpose that work provides for her, and that she feels like a better mother when she is working.

Heather is an Air Force veteran who separated from the military for the sake of her children. After a pregnancy in her teens, she entered the military with the hopes of gaining some discipline and securing a future for herself. Although the military experience was positive for her, she was not willing to sacrifice time away from her children, especially after marrying another military member. Now, as a spouse and recent graduate of nursing school, she is finding it hard to establish a career, and recalls those old feelings of being a teen mom whom nobody expected to succeed.

Michelle Still Mehta

Grace

"The military gave me the freedom to stay home with my kids and not have to justify it to my family or my mom why I wasn't putting my kids in daycare."

Grace is a stay-at-home mom who says being overseas with the military gave her the freedom not to work without having to justify her decision to her family or anyone else. At the same time, with a Master of Business Administration (MBA) and a previous corporate career under her belt, she still believes it's important for her to be a professional role model for her daughters. Grace recalls what it was like in the early years of her marriage, when she and her husband were both working, and she didn't feel like a "real" military spouse yet. During their first assignment at Beale Air Force Base in California, Grace worked as a finance professional for a high-tech company.

When we got married, my husband had just been accepted to medical school. He did medical school through the military, so really there was a great benefit because we had an income during medical school. But I wasn't a *real* military spouse until after his medical school. And after medical school, our first assignment was at Beale Air Force Base.

My first impression of the military was, "Oh, my gosh, I can't believe I'm doing this." We arrived at Beale, and it's brown and empty. And I'm like, "What have we done? Oh, my God. I can't believe we're doing this. There's nothing here, and I'm a city girl. I'm going to shoot myself here." But, I met some wonderful Air Force wives. One, in particular, shaped my experience as an Air Force spouse. She had met my husband the first day there, and she called me on the phone and said, "You have never met me. You don't know who I am. But I met your husband during startup. Do you guys want to go to dinner?" And I was amazed. I was flabbergasted. I thought, "I can't believe this. Who is this nut who

78

is inviting me out to dinner? I mean, how cool, but this is insane."
And it turns out that we've been friends ever since.

So we had friends right away, which was really nice. And then
the rest of the time I worked like crazy. It was my first job after my
MBA. I was earning more money. And I said, "Well, I can do this."
I proved to myself that I can be successful. And I had a cubicle mate
who worked close to me. He was retired military, and he came over
to me and said, "I can't believe you're in the military." I said,
"Why?" He says, "I have never met a military spouse like you."
And I said, "Really?" "Yes, I've never met an *officer's* wife like you."
"Well, what do you mean?" "Well, officers' wives don't work. They
don't have careers. They don't do what you're doing." I'm like,
"Oh, well, I'm different."

I felt mixed [about that], because at that time I'd never really
been a military spouse. I mean, I never really lived on base. I never
shopped on base. I never went to military functions. I didn't have
military friends, except for that lady who called me up, and other
physicians' spouses, who were working too. So, sometimes I kind
of felt proud, like, "Yeah, I'm not what outsiders think of as a
military spouse, some lady who stays at home and is fat and wears
an 'I love the Navy' t-shirt." So I felt good at that time of not being
the typical military spouse. But I kind of felt that [what my
coworker said] was kind of an unfair shot, you know, stereotyping
officers' wives. I knew plenty of officers' wives that weren't snobby
or stuck up.

[I didn't feel like] a military spouse because I didn't do anything
with the military. I rarely went to base. I guess I must have gone
three times a year to the base to visit my husband at the hospital
[where he worked]. Other military wives would take [their
husbands] lunch or dinner. But I commuted [to work] so long that
I would get home at 7:00 p.m. during the week, and there's just no
way that I could go all the way to his office. A lot of the wives
helped their husbands with the out-processing. And I just
couldn't...there was just no way. My husband at one point said,
"These other wives are helping them do this and this." And I said

to him, "You know what, if [my company] was moving me to Europe, would you come and do my paperwork at my job?" He's like, "No." I said, "So, why am I going to go and do your paperwork at your job?"

At this stage in Grace's story, the military is still something she holds a bit at arm's length. She is also honest about holding some deeply negative stereotypes about military spouses. For the most part, she is proud to maintain an identity that does not match this stereotype and to preserve her own career and life separate from the Air Force. That reality is about to change with her first move overseas to Aviano Air Base in Italy.

What happened when you moved to Italy?

My husband and I love to travel. That was one of the reasons that we wanted to go overseas, so we were very excited. And really, work was a secondary thought. Then my boss said, "Okay, just take the job with you."

Initially, it was fine. And I didn't know I was pregnant yet, so that wasn't really a consideration. It was just, "Oh, cool. I can work during the day, and then we can travel during the weekends and things like that." So it was quite comforting to be able to take the work with me. You know, pack up my boxes, and they paid for everything, which was really nice. [My company] sent everything out of my office to my new home. But that was stressful taking my job with me because, in Italy, it's like going from 100 miles an hour down to 10 miles an hour. You've got an Internet hook up, but no data going through. Since I work in finance, you just can't send those kind of files over the Internet. So, yeah, I was kind of frustrated.

It was really difficult, you know. The electricity, for example, you couldn't have three things going at the same time. You couldn't have the dryer going with the computer going with the oven going. All your breakers would pop. And, you know, working in the states is severely multitasking. So I just couldn't multitask, and that was very frustrating. Getting used to that and going to [slower] Italian speed, that was hard actually.

After a short time, Grace discovers that her remote work arrangement from Italy is not viable. Between the time difference and the inadequate technology, she finds the work overwhelming. When she learns she is also pregnant, Grace decides that it does not make sense for her to continue working.

I do have to say my boss was very disappointed [when I quit], because he bent over backward to get me set up and help the military out and to continue my job. When I sent everything back, it was an expense for the company, and it was disappointing for him because it just didn't work out. So I did feel guilty because you're breaking some kind of trust, you know. But, in the end, I thought, "Okay, I'm in Italy now. Have fun." And I found out I was pregnant, so it was going to work out. And working on base never even really seriously crossed my mind because I didn't feel, at that time, that there would be anything available that I would want to do on base, at a level I would want to work at.

I really don't regret stopping working. It was my choice. It was actually kind of liberating, because I don't have any pressure to keep on working and put my kids in daycare. I don't have to justify that to anybody. And, in the states, there are a lot of working moms who look down on stay-at-home moms. I didn't feel I had to justify that to anybody and that was really nice.

I know maybe this sounds strange, but it's easier to justify not working [overseas]. There's really the mentality in the United States, or at least in San Diego [where we were stationed before], that everybody works. And there are very few stay-at-home moms. At least I didn't know any really. So, I didn't have to justify it to my mother. I didn't have to justify it to the rest of my family and tell them why I wasn't working, why I wasn't sticking my kids in daycare. And would I have felt strongly enough or guilty enough to go back to work even if I didn't want to? I don't know. That's not a question I ever had to face. I might have. But then we went to Japan [from Italy]. And then we went to Ramstein.

Ironically, Grace's limited employment opportunities overseas actually feel like a blessing to her. Because she can "justify" not working in places where professional jobs are hard to come by, she feels a relief from the dilemma she might have otherwise faced. Since working does not seem like a viable option, she is free to be the mother she truly wants to be without feeling guilty or ashamed about staying home. Grace's consecutive overseas assignments have enabled her to live the life she wants to live with her family, but now she is beginning to consider what the future may hold. Being a mom has changed her perspective on life and her priorities. What she wanted in the past may be different from what she now wants for her future.

It's only now, when my kids are bigger, that I'm thinking, "What am I going to do now?" I've decided I'm not going to go back to corporate America because I would minimally be gone 7:00 a.m. to 7:00 p.m. I'm going to do something else. I'm going to do a third career. I haven't decided [what] quite yet. I'm looking into teaching, but I'm not sold on it yet. I'm still thinking what I should do.

What would you get out of going back to work?

I think feeling good about myself, a little bit more, again. Also, being a role model for my girls. Having a mom who works is good as a role model. But I just have to be careful. I want to balance. I don't want to just go back to work to earn money. I want to go back to do something that I will like.

Sometimes staying at home is boring, you know? Housework is just absolutely boring. Housework and doing the same routine things, and then driving kids around as a taxi service all the time. At the end of the day you say, "Oh, my God, I have done absolutely nothing today." Though, if you're with me, I'm always in the car. I'm always doing something. I'm always doing something else, but I feel at the end of the day like I've done nothing.

And making your own money is always nice. When I stopped working, I was very clear with my husband. I said, "I'm not going to be working, but the minute that you make me feel bad about not earning money – that is the day I will go back to work and put your kids in daycare." So he said, "No problem." And he is 100% behind what I'm doing, so that has never been an issue. And I always say,

"My money is my money and your money is my money." That's always been our motto in our life. And he's been really cool and supportive about it.

I think just getting out of the house would be nice, spending time for myself with other people who are not children, and talking about different things. That would be really nice. Maybe it's nostalgic. Perhaps, I don't know. Maybe when I get to work I'll be like, "I don't want to talk to any of you guys. I want to go home [and be] with my family."

When Grace talks about the possibility of going back to work, it is clear that she has a desire to strike the right balance in her life. On the one hand, she is unwilling to work a corporate job with demanding hours again and sacrifice time with her family. On the other hand, she does not always find enough fulfillment in the daily life of full-time motherhood. She goes on to explain the importance of being a role model for her daughters.

I think it stems from the fact [that] my mom has always worked. She has a PhD [Doctor of Philosophy degree] and a couple of master's degrees, and I think she associates a lot of value to education and that status. So if I'm not working, some of that role modeling isn't there for the kids. If they choose not to work, that's fine. But I want them to have that role model of going to the university and not feeling bad about being a corporate person if they want to do it, or be a doctor or a whatever, and have that as something normal. Not thinking like, "I should stay at home or be a mom or not go to school because I just want to stay home." I think it's really important to be able to choose, because I see a lot of wives that have children before they finish their education. They're kind of stuck and they don't have education.

I want to make sure that [my daughters] are prepared for that. I think that seeing your mom work or study is a good thing, because it's a good pattern. It's good role modeling. And just seeing me cook and clean and shuttle kids back and forth at this age, it's not something that I want them to do and not have the opportunity to do anything else.

Michelle Still Mehta

I have to say that I do feel now like a *real* military wife because of not working and being in the military. I do feel like our family right now is a military family. So, you look back at the comment that my coworker made, and it fits me. I don't work. Hopefully, I'm not stuck up, but I don't work.

Grace's story comes full circle with her comment about now being a "real" military wife, a role she did not initially see herself playing. Her identity became more integrated into military life as she began to live overseas, and when she decided to leave her corporate career behind, at least temporarily. She is grateful to have the freedom to be the mother she truly wanted to be, a choice she may not have been brave enough to make had she not been enabled by an overseas environment with limited career options. In her case, the barriers to employment that so many spouses face were a blessing in disguise.

Andrea

"As long as I'm not failing, I feel good about it."

Andrea reflects on her transition from the workforce to being a stay-at-home mom. She decided she needed to be home after her first child was born with some serious health problems. Andrea says this decision was difficult at first, but once she started believing that she was doing something important and "not failing," she felt good about her role at home. She begins her story by sharing her background as a college admissions counselor in Virginia, a job she held before she became a mother.

I was an admissions counselor [for a college], so I was helping people get enrolled. And a lot of our enrollments were actually military members. So, for me, that was great, because I could actually talk to them and understand what their concerns were, probably the same concerns I had. And, you know, I was still in school [myself], so in the beginning it was awesome. Here I am, [going to] school, and it was free. [At work] it was the social thing I was really enjoying. And I was really good at the job. I was able to enroll people and get people going, or so I thought.

The job was stressful. At first, I thought it was a stellar company, and then it turned out it was not as good as I thought it was. I want to say 98% of the students I dealt with were military. And, while the college was viewed by the Department of Education as a real school, it didn't have any of the national accreditations. So, I'm starting to hear back from students, "Hey, I tried to transfer [my credits] to another school, but [they're] not transferring because it doesn't have national accreditation." At that point, now I'm feeling bad, because I had gotten military people to sign up for classes that will get them a degree if they stay with us. But if you were looking to get a real education, or transfer [credits] to another school, 9 times out of 10, they're not going to transfer. But to be true to myself and have integrity, especially when it came to other military members, I'm going to be forward and straight up. So I struggled with that for a while.

Integrity comes first. Integrity will always come first, and I will never deliberately mess over a military person. Never. And so I didn't. I told them, "This is what we can do. This is the place that I know it's going to transfer over to. But if you want to go to a nationally accredited school, you need to check with them first because I'm telling you, they may not take [the credits]." I would tell them everything from the beginning, and then my sales numbers started to come back down. And so work got a lot more stressful.

Although Andrea felt conflicted about her work, and the lack of ethical behavior on the part of her employer, she stuck with the job until she had her first child. At that point, not only was the job stressful, but she faced new responsibilities at home, and was quickly consumed by the need to address her daughter's health problems. Compounding the situation, Andrea soon learned they would be moving to Germany, taking her potential return to work off the table for the near future.

I stayed with [that company] until I gave birth to my daughter. I was working for them, and I was going to start working from home; except my daughter initially had a lot of health problems. And I just wasn't able to keep up my job from home. So I resigned.

[I was] kind of sad, because I really did enjoy talking to people all day long. I had some guys, in Korea and Afghanistan, who would use their minutes to call me just to chitchat, because they knew that I would be bright and sunny and made their day better. They started with a stupid question about school and we'd just talk for 20 minutes. I felt bad leaving them because I felt almost like I was abandoning people. But that was how it was.

I wanted to see if things settled down with my daughter, and then maybe I would be able to pick up again with that company, or maybe find another one where I could work from home – just while she was little – but then we moved to Germany.

[My daughter] just kept having all these little [problems]. For the first 6 months, things just weren't quite right. So we just kept going to the doctors, back and forth. At 6 months, she had a really bad problem that she actually was hospitalized for. Three months later, she had a really bad episode where she went catatonic. And we went back to the hospital, but this time they found out that it was an obstruction of the small intestine that had to have surgery. And by that time, I just never did make it to a point where I felt good enough to get someone to help me watch her, or put her into daycare. I just didn't trust anybody else to raise my kid at that point.

During the first 6 months, I just thought I was one of those overparanoid moms. "I need to just back off with her medical stuff. There's nothing wrong with my kid. Stop being a hypochondriac for your daughter." But at 6 months, when I knew I was right [about my daughter's health], it changed everything. Now I'm like, "No, I'm a great mom. And you want to know why? Because I've known this for 6 months and you doctors didn't." Then I felt like a good stay-at-home mom, and this is a real job too. I just don't get paid. So that sort of changed my attitude about it.

Andrea initially questioned herself when she thought something was wrong with her daughter, but this experience taught her the importance of her role as a mother, and to trust her instincts a bit more. Now she believes that being home with her daughter is an important job, but she still wrestles with a sense of social isolation. She misses her own time to get out of the house, go to work, and socialize with other adults.

I was just sort of sad because I'd lost all of those connections at work. I wasn't social. I didn't like it very much, being a stay-at-home mom. It was frustrating. It was lonely. I missed talking. And then, when you do get around to your friends, the only thing you have to talk about is wet diapers. It was very frustrating for me. I've never *not* been able to talk to people before. Because I was the middle of five kids, I don't know how *not* to interact with people. I didn't really have a whole lot, outside of my house or my daughter, going on. So I started doing play groups, and things like that.

87

But it's just not the same. You don't get breaks from the baby; you don't get breaks from the family. And you've got nothing to talk about with a real person anymore. All you know how to do is sing the "Mickey Mouse Clubhouse" song. So it was really frustrating for me. I hate to call work "my time," but it is. I missed having my time. And then, of course, you go through, "Am I a bad mom because I feel this way?"

Tell me more about what you were thinking when you arrived in Germany.

Well, my daughter was getting older. She was about 1½ [years old]. [I thought I'd] put her in the CDC [Child Development Center] a few days a week, and maybe I could find a part-time job somewhere. I hadn't necessarily thought of going back full time, but definitely part time. And then, we got here, and we found out I was pregnant again. I thought, "So, that might not happen." I definitely don't want to be working the first 6 months of his life. Maybe I can still find something I can do from home, but those are more elusive than reality just yet, for me at least. Especially not having finished my bachelor's degree – that makes it harder.

You look around, and your only options really are on base because I don't speak German. And the options on base are very slim because of the fact that all military wives are here. So it's a lot more competitive to get a job on base, at least one that you actually want to have, unless you want to work at the BX or the CDC. I'm not saying anything negative about those jobs, but those are different hours. You can't really plan; you don't know [if or when] you're working Monday through Friday. It could be any time and scheduling things is just a lot harder, especially when you've got a family and you're looking at deployments. And then I just forgot about working through the pregnancy. I'll worry about that later when I can actually do it.

When Andrea found out she was pregnant for the second time, she had to again reframe her expectations. Although she thought she might be ready to return to work, the coming of a second child forced her to reevaluate her plans. Here she describes how she had to come to terms with her ideas about being a stay-at-home mom, and convince herself that she was doing something worthwhile rather than simply failing to be employed. Once she believed that she was not failing, but was actually performing an important job, she began to enjoy her role of motherhood more.

Once I realized I was a good mom, being a stay-at-home mom wasn't the worst thing in the world anymore. I can still talk to people on the phone. I can still do play groups. And to be honest, that's pretty much it. Now I'm an at-home mom. I'd love to have a real job at some point again. Right now, it's just not an option. I don't feel negative about it. I'm actually happy with that decision for now, because I don't feel like I'm a failure. I don't anymore. I did [feel that way during] the first 6 months with my daughter, but at this point, I don't feel like that anymore. I don't like to fail. As long as I'm not failing, I feel good about it.

With my kids, I don't feel like I'm failing because they're getting everything they need from me. I'm teaching them things, at least my daughter anyway. I'm teaching her ABCs, colors, so it is a job in itself because now I'm a teacher. Okay, that's cool. I'm not failing, because I am staying social. I've got new friends here. We've got play groups on Thursdays. We get together and do lunch with our kids, so I'm still being social.

With my daughter, I thought I was failing because I was always taking her to the doctor and not being listened to, which makes you question yourself. If I'm not questioning myself, I'm not failing, because there's nothing to question. The realization [is that] I'm not going to work while they are this little. It just puts the question to rest for now.

And then I can go back and do some classes here and there online, which is what I'm doing now. That will help me get a job later, especially when it's this competitive.

I can't wait to go back to work. I love my kids; I love being an at-home mom, but man, [work would be] time to myself! I know that sounds silly because it's a job, but it's time to myself that I don't have right now. And then I'm contributing to my family too. I can't wait until they're old enough, or at least the baby's old enough for the CDC, or they can go to the German kindergartens. Then I have those hours where I can go have a real job or something. That would be great.

Andrea has adjusted her perspectives on both motherhood and work, based on her first few years as a mother. She has learned the value of her role as a mother, and now accepts her decision to stay home while her two children are of preschool age. Although she misses the social aspects and time to herself associated with working, she is confident the day will come when she is able to return to work and reap those rewards again. In the meantime, she has embraced a healthy view of motherhood that enables her to play the role she wants to play, even if it means putting some of her own needs on the back burner temporarily. The challenge for her in the future will be to remain true to her desires as her children grow.

Tanya

"These have been the worst 3 years of my life."

Tanya is staying home with two toddlers and has mixed feelings about her experience. She wants to work and get out of the house, but doesn't like the thought of outside childcare. She's proud that she's been there for her children, but says it feels like they have been the worst years of her life. Her greatest desire is to work in an administrative role where she could help people keep projects and tasks organized. Before having children, Tanya worked at clerical and temp jobs. She talks about the thrill she gets out of organizing things for other people, a thrill she does not get out of daily household tasks and caretaking.

If I actually had a career, I would make sure it was in something that I've been studying for, which is essentially a glorified secretary. Every business in the world needs a secretary of some sort, so I know I won't have a shortage of opportunities to find a job. It's just the way my mind works. I can focus on weird, menial tasks – stuffing envelopes, typing, stacking, collating, and organizing. That's just the way I like to work. I don't have any opportunity to do that right now. I mean, I can organize my kids' clothes into color-coded stacks but that's about all I get right now.

These have been the worst 3 years of my life. I mean, I love my kids, but I've basically been pregnant and/or nursing since we got here [to Germany]. I love my girls, but I want to get away from them for a few hours every day at least. And if I get a job [at] the Exchange or the Commissary, my paycheck's going to pay for their daycare. So I'm doing one thing to pay for another.

When I initially got here, I had about a month left in my [community college] classes, so I didn't really look for anything at that point. I'd already been awarded a [security] clearance, so I was thinking, "Okay, I'll try to get a job, maybe at the hospital, or just any kind of secretary job." It didn't have to be anything fancy. But

Michelle Still Mehta

I was waiting until I finished my schooling so I could say, "I have an associate degree." At that point, I found out I was pregnant and thought, "Do I really want to do that to an employer? Do I want to get in, get trained, and have all these appointments that I'm going to all the time?" So I said, "I'll wait. I'll have my kid, get through the maternity leave stage, and then I'll look." And, by that time, I was so tired from my daughter, and my husband was always at work. He's a typical dad. He'll change a diaper, he'll feed them, but when they cry, it's, "Go see your mother." My expectations of what I thought I would be doing over here [in Germany] definitely have fallen through.

Like Andrea, Tanya decided she had to change her expectations about working when she became a mother. She liked the idea of working, but decided it didn't make sense to work once she examined the trade-offs, both financially and emotionally. Financially, she was concerned that the jobs available to her would not adequately cover the cost of childcare, let alone generate a second income. Emotionally, she realized that the sacrifice she would be making by losing time with her children during their formative years was too great. The conflict she feels about this is clear as she claims it was "an easy call," but then goes on to say she began submitting job applications once her baby was 3 months old.

It was a choice between staying home and taking care of my kid versus working. It was an easy call, because I didn't want to let somebody else raise my kid and throw them in the CDC or whatever. Then you get to see all those moments. I get to see the first steps or the first tooth, all that. I didn't want to give up all that and give the moments to somebody else.

Those first 3 months when you nurse and the child will get all the antibodies from the breast milk and everything – I wanted to get through that without having to worry about having to pump and everything. And once I got to that stage, I started filling out applications online and submitting resumes. I just never got any call backs.

I went on the USAJOBS website and the Service's [Army and Air Force Exchange Service] website and I just [applied for] anything clerical, office automation, administrative assistant, anything in that generalized category. Either they hired other people or I wasn't clicking all the right boxes to get the spousal preference.[9] I don't know. I never got any notifications back on any of them, so I never got a reason why I wasn't selected. I was very discouraged.

I thought, "Hey, I already have this clearance. That's $5,000 they're not going to have to spend on me to get it covered. That should give me a little boost up, and I have this degree..." And, nothing, so it was just, "Okay, great. I feel worthless."

About the time I just kind of gave up on it, I found out I was pregnant with my second child. And then we were also trying to move out of our off-base house because our landlady was not being pleasant. I was searching online trying to find houses, trying to take care of my first child, and it just consumed my time. Plus, I was trying to finish up a second associate [degree], and starting to work on my bachelor's. So everything just had me preoccupied, and I didn't really have time to think about trying to find a job.

Right now, we're looking to get my oldest signed up for German preschool in the fall, and then the following year my second daughter will be able to go into preschool. Hopefully, at that point, I'm going to try and get my resume looking really nice so I can start submitting it for jobs.

---

[9] "Spousal preference" refers to the DoD's Priority Placement Program (PPP) that is intended to give military spouses preference in federal hiring. Under this program, military spouses can receive hiring preference for federal jobs but can only utilize that preference once per assignment. For more information about the PPP, contact your local Civilian Personnel Office or see Military OneSource: https://www.militaryonesource.mil. This topic will come up again later in this chapter.

For the most part, knowing that I've been there for [my kids] and that I've been there through everything makes me feel good. But there are just those days when I want to say, "Somebody, come take them." I've been getting a little stir crazy, sitting at home when they're asleep. I don't want to make any noise, because then they're going to wake up and then I'm not going to get anything done. So I just sit there and quietly type on my homework right now. Stir crazy would probably be the best way to describe it.

Tanya's explanation of events in her life demonstrates the pull she feels to both work and be home with her children. She is frustrated that she has not successfully landed a job, but also seems unsure if she would be prepared to take a job if it means placing her children in childcare. Like Andrea, she admits that the daily life of full-time motherhood is not as fulfilling as she would like, but seems less willing to accept this reality than Andrea was. Tanya is still searching for a way to resolve her inner conflict and be the mother she thinks she should be while still having some outlet for herself outside the home. Here, she explains what she misses most about working in an office.

Just the constant work flow, something that I could always be doing. Whether it's typing up the minutes from a meeting, typing up a report, proofreading somebody else's paper, or emailing. Just something that I could be focused on for 5 or 6 hours out of the day, where I'm helping people, helping get tasks done that need to be done that nobody else wants to do. I know I'm crazy for it, but I like that kind of thing. I like the hard tasks that nobody else wants to do. The one that everybody goes, "Oh, I have to do *that* again." Those kinds of tasks.

I think for me it's the same as when people jump out of airplanes and go bungee jumping or ride roller coasters. That's their kind of thrill. For me, it's taking on those jobs that nobody wants to do. It's not exactly a thrill, but it's the same kind of feeling. I don't know a better way to describe that.

I like it because then I know I accomplished something. I can see the physical results of the work, especially when it's stacking, organizing, and everything. When you see the mess, and then you see the organization, everybody can find everything. That just makes me feel better, which is good. Everybody can say, "Oh, I need a…" And it's there. They don't have to dig through a drawer, look in a box. They can find exactly what they need, right in front of them.

When I organize or straighten things up at home, then my husband comes home and can't find anything. And then he and I get into an argument about why I put this there when it should go here. So I don't get the thanks at home that I would get from a job. I don't know. For whatever reason, if I'm outside of the house, the tedium and the repetition doesn't bother me.

When I'm in the house, it wears on me more because I've been stuck in the house for the last 3 years. It's like, "Great, laundry. But I just did laundry yesterday, and I don't want to do laundry today. Now I have to do dishes." It wears on me; but if I had a job, I'd have that break from the house and the dishes and the laundry and the tedium. So I could switch back and forth between the two.

It's kind of the way some grandparents feel about their grandkids. They love to have them, but they're so glad when they get to give them back. Same thing at a job. You love the work, but you can leave it there and take a break from it. I need the break from the house. That's what I'm looking for.

Like many military spouses with young children, Tanya finds herself in a bind. She believes she is doing the right thing by staying home, and that working may not be practical for the time-being, but emotionally she feels stuck and "stir crazy." The role of mother seems to trump everything else for her, but eventually she will need to reconcile her personal desires with her desires for her children. While her toddlers may need her complete energy and attention now, she will need to find room for her own goals if she is going to be satisfied in the long run. Figuring out where and when employment fits into that picture is essential for her, but only she can decide what the right answer will be.

Michelle Still Mehta

Katie

"It's like I'm a married, single mom."

Katie is a pilot's wife and former athletic trainer who now calls herself a "married, single mom." Although she believes her role as a mom is important, she acknowledges that losing the professional part of herself has been a painful sacrifice. Before having children, Katie worked as a high school athletic trainer and loved her job. She expected to be able to maintain her career as a military spouse and mother, but the combination of military moves, parenting demands, and a frequently absent husband turned out to be incompatible with her career plans. Katie begins her story by describing what her work meant to her in the early years of her marriage, before kids.

I lived, breathed, and ate athletic training. My goal was to try to get the athletes as healthy as possible and keep them healthy. It was a high school setting, yet they were my kids. I took them underneath my wing and just made sure that they were okay. So it was neat. If my kids got hurt, I was hurt. It was rewarding to know the athletes could step onto the field and know that they are sound.

I knew I was marrying into the Air Force. So I knew what I was kind of getting into. And he knew my job schedule. If it was cross country season, I'd get up at 5:00 in the morning, be at school at 5:30, and I'd come home at 7:30 or 8:00 p.m., depending on if basketball or football was going on. So I had long days as well. We kind of knew he had long days and I had long days. So it kind of meshed, it worked.

And that's when September 11th happened and I was like, "Okay, my job is not as important as my husband's." For 3 days I couldn't get in touch with him. Finally, he got a hold of me and told me to meet him at the house that weekend and we would pack. And then he would be gone.

September 11, 2001, was a pivotal time in Katie's military life and marriage. She says this was the point she first realized her husband's job

96

was more important than hers. This moment seems to mark a shift in her understanding of military life and what it will be like to be a military spouse in the days following the attacks of September 11th. Although she still believes maintaining her career is achievable, she is beginning to see the challenges ahead of her as a military spouse and, eventually, mother.

At that time, while I was working at [the high school], the principal's husband was prior military. She sat down and talked to me a little bit about what it meant to be a military spouse. She said it's a hard life and there are lots of sacrifices by the spouse. I kind of knew that, but I thought it wouldn't be that hard because I had my own life. I still have my job, all the teams I take care of. I was like, "Okay, I can do this."

I thought it would be pretty easy, which it kind of was, until you have a child. When we got to Charleston [South Carolina], I thought, "As soon as she is born, I'll get her into a school, a preschool, or some kind of daycare, and then I'll go back to work." But because of what happened after September 11th, he was gone 2 weeks and then home for maybe 1 or 2 days [for] crew rest, and then he'd turn around and go again for 2 weeks. So there was never an opportunity for me to put my feet back into that world. But, you know, I maintained my credentials. And I still have a passion for it, [but] my career got put on the backside.

When Katie's career gets "put on the backside," she begins to sort out how she will handle this reality. She explains how she compensated with some volunteer work and focused on being a good mother, but was still frustrated by the demands placed on her husband and the feeling that there was no room for her to do anything to further her own career. She also had to come to terms with her own feelings of ambivalence about being a stay-at-home mom, after being raised by a mother who did not work.

I went up to the athletic training room there at Centenary College [when we were in Charleston], and I would help out. I would volunteer, but I didn't get paid for it. It was so weird because I've never just sat. I'm always constantly going, and then all of a sudden, I'm like, "Oh, it's too quiet. I need to go do something." So that's when I would just go up and volunteer at the school. I did that for a couple of months, and then my husband was picked up for pilot training.

He said, "I'm going to become a pilot and I'm going to be gone. But, you know, you can still work." I thought I would always get back in it because it's a passion [of mine]. I know there's a few women who do it. My sister works and her husband works, but he comes home at night. He's there on the weekends. We don't always have that luxury. So with his unpredictable schedule, it's hard for me to work. It's a challenge, and I haven't gotten back into it.

My mom stayed home with us. And it was like, "What do you do, Mom? You stay home and take care of us. That's not a big job." But, now that I'm a mom, I look back and go, "Wow, that was a huge job she did for us and [it was] a sacrifice as well." Now I'm looking at my daughter and I'm like, "Oh, you think your mom is a slacker because she doesn't work." She doesn't quite get it; but she does get it, to some extent, that moms do work.

It's like I'm a married, single mom. That's the term I always use. I'm married, but I'm a single mom because he's always gone. So I have to raise the two kids by myself. At first, it was shock, total shock. And then I didn't want to leave my children. The gears started switching. I didn't want to go back to work because I didn't want to leave this baby for somebody else to raise. So that's when I told my husband [that] I'll stay home a year and then I'll get back to work. And then the pace did not stop. It got to be where he was also deploying, and it went from 45 days to 90 days, and then 3-week TDYs. And then he'd come home for 2 or 3 days and then he'd go again. So my priorities were slipping, yet the desire was still there. I was like, "Okay, one day, I can still do this." That's what I kept telling myself, "One day..." But when is this one day coming? [It feels like] it was a sacrifice, one worth making, but it was a sacrifice.

Katie paints a picture of a gradually shifting set of expectations and roles rather than a sudden change or decision point in her career. As her husband's travel and work demands intensified, she felt her priorities "slipping." Ultimately, the value she places on being available to her children overrides her career desires and, in her mind, that justifies the sacrifice she has made. Yet, she goes on to say that this sacrifice has come at a real cost to her personally.

I lost a part of myself as a person because [my job was] how I identified myself. [It's what] I thought I was supposed to be and supposed to be doing, and that's what I worked hard to do. And I do mean blood, sweat, and tears. I worked so hard for that. So it is a very painful sacrifice. But then look what I gained. I lost that part of me but I gained two children, two beautiful, healthy children. And I have a wonderful husband. So I'm like, "Okay, God, this is good. If this is where you want me, okay. But can I still have a little bit of that?"

My job, my career, does not exist. My career is being an Air Force wife. My career is being that spouse that is behind my husband, taking care of the kids on the sideline, and making sure that when he comes home, everything is taken care of; and there's really nothing for him to do, except balance the checkbook. I cannot balance a checkbook to save my life. But I can do everything else. So that's what my role is now. And it's one I do not mind. I'm proud of my husband, and I'm proud of the military and what they're doing. So it's a small sacrifice that I can do for them.

I thought I was a strong individual, but this has made me stronger. [I know now] that I can take care of a house, and all the things that break on it, with my husband being gone. I can take care of issues that I never thought I would have to take care of by myself. There's independence there, so it's kind of a double-edged sword.

Katie is proud to support her family and knows in her heart that she has made good decisions for the sake of being a good mother to her children. At this stage in her life, it is unclear if that sacrifice is a temporary one or if her career aspirations will always stay on the "backside." Ultimately, that will depend on her ability to manage the competing roles in her life, not only as a mother, but also as a wife and military spouse.

Michelle Still Mehta

Isabelle

"I realized who I am and who I'm not."

Isabelle has an established contracting career in the GS system, and is a newly married military spouse. Saying the "grass in not always greener," she talks about her decision to keep working even though she used to long for the opportunity to stay home when she was a single parent. Once she had the option to stay home, she realized that home life was not all she thought it would be, and that being a working mother is the right answer for her.

I married my husband right before we moved here [to Germany]. So this is our first duty station together. I met my husband about 2 weeks after I finished my master's degree. Prior to that, I had no time to date or do anything because I was working on my degree. I was a single parent. I was also doing what I do now. I'm a contract specialist for the government. At that time, I was working for a DoD agency. We met and got engaged very quickly, and then he got orders to come here. I was looking for opportunities outside of the organization I was working at because I had finished my master's degree and was looking for something else.

So it was very quick. He got his orders in December. I decided in January to go with him. And then we were gone in February. So I didn't have time to look for a job. And, as a matter of fact, I was kind of looking forward to not having a job for a while, because I had not done that. I had my daughter [from a previous relationship] when I was 20 and worked every day since then. And I was thinking, "Oh, this is going to be nice to have a break!" So we got here and we went to the newcomers' briefing, and Civilian Personnel had a table set up. My husband went over and he was talking to them about what I do. And they said, "Oh, we have so many vacancies for that. Are you interested in starting to work?" And I thought, "I know how it is with the government employment

100

process." I thought, "Yeah, okay," knowing that it would take a while. But I got an offer 2 days later.

Isabelle was initially excited to have a break from work for the first time in her life, but then found herself going back to work much sooner than she expected. She wasn't sure she wanted to stay in the contracting field either, but explains that she didn't want to lose her military spouse preference by turning down the offer she received.

Now that I had my master's degree, I thought maybe I could move into a different career, something similar, still something with business, not psychology, but maybe something a little bit more *me*. I was putting in for jobs across the country, even across the world, still thinking it's just me and my daughter. But then I got married and came over here. I guess I could have not worked or waited to find the perfect job, but I don't think there's a lot of perfect jobs at my level in the GS system. So, I got into contracting again.

If I didn't accept that job, I could not use my military spouse preference again, so I took it. It wasn't necessarily what I would have chosen on my own if I was the one picking where I want to work or what I want to do.

What was it like in those first few weeks before you started working again?

[I had] the idea of not working because, since my daughter was born, I've worked full time. And I thought, "Oh, this is going to be great. I'll take her to school in the morning and then I'll come home. I'll make her snacks and I'll pick her up from the bus stop." I was very excited about that stay-at-home mom aspect that I've never gotten to do. And then, when I started doing that, I thought, "This really isn't for me." She'd come home and I'd have her cute little snack that I worked all day on and she'd say, "Can I go play over at my friend's house?" And I'd be like, "Okay, bye." So it wasn't what I envisioned it was going to be.

[I thought] that we would spend time together and go for walks and we would bake. Just those things that you want to do with your children when you're stuck at work and you think, "Oh, if I was at home this is what I'd be doing." But the reality of it was she was at school all day. My husband was working very long hours, and when we first moved here, we only had the one car. So he would take the car and I'd be stuck unpacking boxes all day long [with] no TV, nothing to do, no friends. She'd come home, "Mom, I want to go play with my friends down the street." And I could have been at work interacting with people. I guess that's what I thought I was going to be doing at home. Instead of interacting with customers and people, I'd have my family to interact with. But I didn't even have that.

I realized who I am and who I'm not. I spent 8 years wishing that my life was different, that I could stay home. And I think that really helped me realize that the grass isn't always greener [on the other side]. That's not who I am. It's not like you see on TV where you're in the kitchen with your daughter and you guys are baking and having fun. It's not that way. So [this experience] really helped me to go back to work and not be wishing that I was at home. But that didn't last long, because when I have bad days at work I think, "Gosh, if I was at home right now…"

Later on, I took an entire summer off [from work] because my son was born in the beginning of the summer. For the first month I was like, "Oh, I want to do this. I don't want to go back to work." And then it got to that third month and I was deciding every day whether I should bathe. And my daughter is still wanting to go hang out with her friends. I love my son, but all day long it's just me and him, and I thought, "Yeah, this isn't it. I need more interaction."

It's not like I need to be around people all the time, but I need to be around people *sometimes*. I need to have some adult interaction. I guess it wouldn't be so bad if my husband was not working such late hours or TDY all the time. But I would go 3 or 4 days and realize I hadn't spoken to another adult. And I need that on a daily basis. I need to have motivation to get up in the morning and bathe and brush my teeth and have a plan. And I think, if left to my own devices, I would not do those things. If I didn't have a reason [to do something else], I would probably sit in my living room and play with my baby all day long, and slowly get fat and not bathe. I need motivation to do something.

Isabelle had often longed for the opportunity to stay home with her children, but realized that the reality of staying home did not match her expectations. In fact, she preferred the interaction she got from working to the solitude and lack of structure she often felt being at home. As she goes on to explain, the structure and achievement she derived from work was important to her. Furthermore, she believes that the time she spends with her children is better spent when she is working because it is "quality" time versus "quantity" time. In her eyes, there is no conflict between working outside the home and being a good mother.

I feel, for the most part, I'm accomplishing things [at work], and I think everyone needs to feel like [that] at the end of the day. I need to look back and say, "This is what I did today. This is who I helped today." If I have a day where I think I didn't do anything or accomplish anything, it's kind of sad for me. So when I'm working, I feel like at the end of the day I have a story to tell my daughter at the dining room table, something funny to tell my husband. Otherwise, you spend the day at home and it's like, "What do you have to talk about?" "Nothing. I did laundry today." So it's a sense of accomplishment, I guess.

Long term, if that were my life plan to stay home, I just don't think I would feel like I accomplished much. Of course, I would be raising my children and spending all day with them. And I hate to make it sound like I don't want to do that. I absolutely enjoy the time that I spend with them. But I think going to work and spending the day not with them, means the time that I do have with them is quality time. When I would spend all day with them, it's kind of like, "Well, we have all day to fit in all the fun stuff we could do." And now, we have 3 hours. So I make it a point to do what I can do with my daughter in that time or on the weekends. We make sure that we pack it full of fun things so that it's quality time since we don't have the quantity of time.

How do you think being a military spouse affects your career?

On my own, I had done very well and people looked to me as being an expert. And then I come [to Germany] and get hired as a spouse [through the PPP]. [With PPP] they don't even look at your resume. They make sure you're qualified. Then you hit the list, meaning you're qualified, and then they have to pick you [over other candidates].[10]

Maybe it's not this way everywhere, but I've heard from other spouses that are in the GS system that this is typical: You come into work [as a spouse-preference hire] and you're given the lowest duties, no matter what your capabilities are, because the expectation is, "She's just a spouse. She's a 'stopper.' She stopped me from getting [or hiring] the person I really wanted."

I'm not knocking the effort, because it is great that they make an effort to put a program in place to hire spouses. But knowing my experience – where I came in and had this experience, had this level of appreciation, and was really looked at as an expert in my last place – and then coming here [where] people don't ask you a single question about your expertise. They just give you the smallest duty that they could possibly give you so that you won't mess it up. It didn't take very long for them to realize [that] I know what I'm doing. But I feel like now, every time I move, this is something that I have to prove.

Every time [I move], I'll just have to prove myself and that is really going to impact my ability to promote. When I came here, I had been a GS-11 for quite a while in my old agency, and was being looked at for promotions. But I came here as a military spouse preference GS-11. If I leave here as a GS-11, I'll get stuck as a GS-11 somewhere else and have to prove myself again. By the time I do, it'll be time to move again, stuck as a GS-11 again.

---

[10] Isabelle's explanations of the Priority Placement Program are based on her personal experience, and may not be a completely accurate reflection of current policy.

My mom was a spouse and my dad was in the military. She retired as a GS-7 because they moved, sometimes every year, during his career. And I never understood why it was so hard for her. A lot of times she just didn't even want to work because she had to start fresh every time. And I get it now. I get it. I realize I have to take more ownership of my career. And that's why I started looking external to my squadron. And, hopefully, when we move this time, we'll have more notice and I can start putting in for jobs that won't even know that I'm a spouse. I'll just have to try to get a job on my own. Honestly, I probably won't use the spouse preference program again.

I think I'm at a level where I could get a job on my own. It wouldn't be as easy. It certainly wouldn't take [just] 2 days to get an offer. It would take longer. But I would prefer for somebody to hire me looking at my resume and knowing what I'm capable of than to get hired faster just because of the spouse [preference] program. I do think that it's great for entry-level spouses because that's how you're treated anyway, as an entry-level person that doesn't know anything.

I guess I have a little bit of bitterness because I feel like I've already proven myself. I can stand on my own. And now it's not me. It's Sergeant X's wife. That's who I am now, even in my own career. And that's so weird to me. It's not a bad thing. I'm very involved in all the spouses' groups. The second day we were here, I went to a spouses' meeting and it was the same thing. "What does your husband do?" was the first question. "Who's your husband?" Not, "What do *you* do?"

I'm not knocking it, you know. I'm very proud of my husband, but it seems like military spouses – at least the one's I've encountered – tie their identity very close to what their husband does, and who he is. But that's not me. And it certainly doesn't reflect where I'm at in my career.

[Being a military spouse has] really made me question things that I thought I knew about myself, just what my values were. I always just put my interests first, my career first. And I'm very surprised at how easy it is *not* to do those things [anymore]. People say all the time it's weird that I'm following him around rather than him following my career, because I'm further into my career [than he is into his]. My career is still important, just not as important as I always thought it was. And I know that one of the reasons my career was important was because I needed to keep making money to support my daughter. And it's not so necessary now that I'm not living on one income.

Isabelle's role has changed from single mother to married military spouse and mother; this shift has reframed her outlook on working and motherhood. Where she used to be jealous of mothers who could stay home, she now realizes that model of motherhood doesn't work for her. She continues to work; however, it is no longer out of necessity but out of choice, which makes her feel like a burden has lifted. For the first time in her life, she is able to freely choose the right mix of working and motherhood for her.

Heather

"I'm following him around and trying to fit in where I can."

Heather recently achieved her lifelong dream of finishing nursing school and becoming a nurse, but can't find paid work in Germany. She is proud of overcoming the hardship of starting out as a teen mom, but is now frustrated that she isn't able to work. A former member of the Air Force herself, she separated from the military because she believed it was in the best interest of her marriage and her children.

I was in the Air Force. I was actually a single mom. I got pregnant at 16, had a baby at 17. And in order for me to join the Air Force, I had to give temporary custody to my mom, because you cannot join the Air Force and be a single parent. So I gave temporary custody to my mom with the hopes of him [my son] coming back with me once I finished tech school. I felt that the Air Force was going to better myself career wise. I had gotten my certified nursing assistant license and I was a general receptionist for a couple of years. I just kind of felt like I was going nowhere with my career, so I decided the Air Force was probably best for me. Plus, I needed some discipline, so I joined the Air Force.

Then I met my husband, and we knew the chances of us getting assigned [together] weren't good. At that point, I knew he and I were going to get married, and I just felt that the best interest was for me to get out. So that's what I did.

[Being in the Air Force] was definitely a self-esteem booster at the time. But at the same time, I was separated from my son. It was always "service before self," and I thought, "I'm sorry, but I'm not putting service before my kid." That is what it kind of came down to. I was using the Air Force as a stepping stone to further my career. I always knew I wanted to go into the nursing field, but being a single mom and trying to do it was just difficult. I felt like it definitely gave me the self-confidence that I needed though.

I don't know if it was the discipline. I mean, my dad was retired military with 24 years in the Air Force, and so I was already used to the ways of the military. It just made me feel a little more at home. [My time in] high school was the longest I had ever lived anywhere. All my life we moved every 4 or 5 years. So maybe it just made me feel a little more comfortable and relaxed because it was more structured.

Tell me what happened after you got out of the Air Force and got married.

Actually, I was pregnant and I still knew I wanted to be in the medical field. I always had that desire. So I started looking for work and I found a job at a radiology department in Washington, DC. I did medical assisting there all the way through my pregnancy. And then, our oldest was 5 at the time. My husband was only a senior airman, and we lived in DC. It wasn't a good area of town, so we were paying for one to go to private school so he wouldn't go to the horrible schools in DC. So I was kind of iffy if I wanted to go back to work at that point, but I decided money wise it wasn't going to be worth it for daycare and private school. I always wanted to be a stay-at-home mom anyway so it was like, "You know what? I can put my career on hold and do what I've got to do." So I never went back to work then at the radiology department after I had my baby.

Heather's story outlines all the reasons why it made sense for her to stop working and stay home with her young children. Remaining on active duty seemed like too much of a sacrifice for her and her family. By the time her second child came along, civilian employment did not seem appropriate either. It felt like the right time in her life to be a stay-at-home mom, a decision she stands by. However, this decision did come at some cost as she describes her feeling of lost independence and a desire to eventually go back to nursing school.

It was hard at first because I had always been independent. I mean, at the age of 16, I always paid my own car payment, paid my own insurance. I got a job right at 15½, as soon as I could in Virginia. So it was kind of hard for the first time to have somebody pay my bills. You know what I mean? And my husband would be like, "Look, you're going to have to understand we're married now and what's mine is yours and vice versa." It just was the best thing, financially, for us. And, emotionally, I felt good because I've always been the independent one, and for once somebody was taking care of me.

I don't know exactly when it happened, but my husband had his career and was working on getting his bachelor's degree. I'm like, "Gosh, if anything were to happen and we would not be together, I don't really have any skills." I felt like he was getting his education but I was the one staying home, just with mommy skills. So I think probably right after we were in Okinawa [Japan], I said, "Okay, I've got to do something with my education. I've got to go back to school." I don't want to say it's a jealousy thing, but maybe I'm envious. You're envious of their career.

So I started doing my prerequisites for nursing in Okinawa. And that felt good. That was like, "Woo-hoo! I'm doing something for me finally."

This part of Heather's story demonstrates the intersection between motherhood and military life. Although she originally stopped working in order to stay home with her children, the main obstacle she now faces to employment has to do with the frequent relocation inherent to military life. Just as she was prepared to restart her career, she found herself moving overseas to Germany.

In Florida, I finished the rest of my prerequisites and got accepted into a nursing program there. But the thing you're worried about the whole time is, "Okay, I hope we don't get orders, hope we don't get orders." And then, before I even finished, this assignment came open in March and my husband was like, "Should we put in for it? It's my dream job." We wanted to go to Germany. He was stationed in Germany before we met.

I was like, "Well, am I going to be able to get a job?" That was my top priority. I worked my butt off for this. I want to be able to

109

work. And I actually called Landstuhl [Regional Medical Center][11] from the states and inquired, and they were like, "Well, it might be tough. You might have to volunteer first, but try to get as much experience there." So we put in for the assignment with the hopes that we would get it. I just left it in God's hands and figured if it was meant to be, we would get it. If it wasn't meant to be, then we would stay there until we got another assignment. And then we found out just 2 weeks later.

So then I graduated and it was like, "Okay, well we don't leave until September. What do I do in the meantime?" So I ended up taking a job and not telling them we were PCSing because number one, I needed the experience, and number two, I didn't know if we were going to get the [medical] clearance for our son because of his medical history. So I figured I'll take the job because our orders could get canceled.

I had a job at a hospital in Tampa [Florida]. I was very excited about it. As soon as we definitely got the orders and got the A-Okay, I just let them know and they were fine. Having that job, that was *good*. That was the first time I had a paycheck in 10 years. I mean, I know that his money is our money but it was *my* first paycheck. So it was good. It was definitely rewarding, and ever since I can remember, I always knew I wanted to be a nurse. So I thought, "Okay, this is a real thing."

Now I'm volunteering on the mother-baby unit [at Landstuhl], and it took months to get on there. It just kind of stinks. You have this dream all your life and something you want to do, and we were finally at the location we want to be, and I can't get a [paid] job.

You're giving all this education and experience for free, but there's only so long you want to do it [because] you're not getting paid. I just remember one of the colonels coming in and saying, "This hospital wouldn't run without our volunteers, and they save us a hundred and something million dollars a year." That's great

---

[11] Landstuhl Regional Medical Center (LRMC) is a U.S. military hospital in Landstuhl, Germany, not far from Ramstein.

and all, but they're in desperate need. They need more nurses to come forward, but they don't have the positions. They don't have the funding to do it. They just continue to take volunteers. Somebody said to me the other day, "Well, why do you even volunteer? That's just less of a chance for you to get a job when they're getting all this free work." Well, I need the experience. I need the continuing education. So I guess it's double sided.

What is it that you want to get out of working? Why is it important to you?

I think self-gratification. It just makes you feel better as a person. You feel like you've done your share to help someone else out. I feel bad for my husband, too, because he makes those little comments like, "I wish I could stay home." I'm like, "No, you don't! I wish I could work. I'll trade spots with you. I'll go in and you stay home for the day." I want to be able to contribute even though we share everything. I want to be able to have extra money. I want to be able to have a savings account. I want to be able to not live paycheck to paycheck, which is what we've done for 10-plus years. And that's a big thing. And, of course, you're in Europe. You want to be able to travel and go places and do stuff. It's the chance of a lifetime here. Oh, my gosh, I wish I had a job!

I may have to go back to just being a receptionist somewhere. You go to school for all these years to try to finally get your degree, and then it's like, well, there are jobs at the CDC. You feel like you're almost taking a step down, but what do you do?

It definitely makes me feel like crap, having [a degree] and not being able to use it. You work hard for something and then it just kind of sits there and collects dust, which is what I feel like my education is doing. It's funny because I remember when I was at orientation, I met a couple of girls who said, "If I can't get a job here, I'm just going back to the states and then will come see my husband every couple of months." And I thought, "I'm sorry, but that's not happening." Where the Air Force sends my husband is where he sends all of us. We're going together as a family, and that's what you have to do. You have to make do and it's his career. I'm following him around and trying to fit in where I can.

It stinks though. I told my husband, joking, "Okay, when you retire in the next couple of years, you're going to follow me. I'm going to take jobs all over the United States and you're going to have to follow me and find a job wherever." He jokes and says he'll be a stay-at-home dad. He's definitely good and he's been very supportive.

How has this experience in Germany impacted you?

It definitely is a blow to your self-esteem because you start getting proficient in something and you have confidence, but you can't do what you set out to do. It definitely makes you feel horrible. *Heather is crying.* You want to do something better with yourself. All my life I've [been] labeled as the teen mom who's not going to amount to anything. I've finally gotten over this huge label and then you really can't do anything with it. So maybe I shouldn't even have gone to school. Maybe it was just a waste.

Heather is frustrated by her situation, while trying to remain hopeful and motivated. She has invested a great deal in her nursing education and is on the brink of starting a brand new career. Unfortunately, she has to be patient enough to see how her story will unfold. Will her volunteer efforts turn into a paid position? How long will she have to wait to land the nursing job that she longs to have? How many more obstacles will military life put in her way? In some ways, this is a typical story of a mother reentering the workforce after taking a break to stay home. These women may find that they have to reinvest in new education or start at entry-level positions to make up for lost time. Heather is finding there is some cost associated with the time she spent at home, compounded by the challenges created by military moves and living overseas. As the next chapter demonstrates, military life can be a challenge for even the most tenacious military spouses.

Lessons on Motherhood

What do the stories in this chapter tell us about motherhood? Do you see yourself in any of these portraits? Here are a few lessons I hope you will take away from this chapter:

1. **Only you can define what being a good mother means to you.** We all know that parenting comes with no rulebook, and there are as many different ways to be a parent as there are parents. Yet, it seems that women, in particular, care a great deal about what other people think of their parenting. We seek advice and role models from our own mothers, friends, colleagues, blogs, articles, etc. We may participate in that long-standing feud between working mothers and stay-at-home mothers who harshly judge each other for choosing the less enlightened parenting path. Grace talks about this eloquently when she describes the freedom she feels being able to stay at home while living overseas without being judged negatively by her peers or mother.

   The most powerful lesson I've learned from these stories of motherhood is that nobody but you can decide what good mothering means to you. Grace is grateful for the freedom to stay home, while Isabelle learned that staying home did not make her a better mother. After buying into the idea for so long that life would be better if she could only stay home, when given the chance to do so, she realized that wasn't true for her. Both Grace and Isabelle are right in their points of view, and happier, because they have chosen to follow the best path for themselves and their families.

2. **Stay-at-home moms need rewards and recognition too.** Employers know they have to keep employees motivated to retain them and keep them happy. They need to know they are appreciated and performing well. Stay-at-home moms

113

are no different, except that they have no employer and they don't get paid. They are the ultimate self-motivated worker, and it is no wonder they sometimes feel undervalued and unappreciated. Andrea shares that she felt like a failure staying home until she began to see it as her new full-time job. Once she reframed her role as her children's teacher, she began to see worth in what she was doing every day and no longer felt like she was failing. On the flip side, Tanya loves to organize things but gets no satisfaction from doing that at home because she does not earn the recognition she would enjoy at an office job. Without the recognition that she longs for, Tanya is missing the motivation she needs to feel good about getting her work done. Andrea is able to find that motivation internally, while Tanya is looking for external validation.

3. **The choice to stay home can create a painful loss of professional identity.** Katie talks extensively about the sacrifice she made by giving up her athletic training career to stay home with her children. Although she does not regret her decision, she admits she has lost a big piece of herself that she would like to get back someday. For her, giving up that professional side of herself is not as much about employment as it is about identity and meaning. She wants to regain a part of herself that is now missing. Although she is proud of raising her children, she also recognizes that they may not believe her job as a mother is very important. In sacrificing so much for her children, Katie has become a little less whole herself.

4. **Military life is a good fit for stay-at-home moms, which can be a double-edged sword.** As Grace explains in her story, moving overseas with the military enabled her to justify her decision to stay home and raise her young children. Because employment can be so difficult at

overseas assignments, staying overseas was a perfect fit with her desire to be home. Her vision of motherhood was compatible with military life. Unfortunately, that same scenario can lead other military spouses to stay home reluctantly when they would prefer to work. For example, Heather worked hard to finish nursing school and get back into the workforce, but has been unable to land a paid position in an overseas location. She now finds herself a stay-at-home mom once again, fueling her insecurities about being a teen mom who never thought she would amount to much.

5. **Military spouses face the same challenges that civilian working mothers face, but military life intensifies those challenges.** Many of the parenting challenges described in this chapter are not unique to military life. Like civilian women, these spouses have grappled with conflicting feelings about staying home versus working, whether or not to use childcare services, and how to strike the right balance between working and parenting. However, the military spouses in these stories also simultaneously faced overseas moves, husbands who deployed or left frequently for TDYs, and all the uncertainties associated with military life. As Katie accurately describes it, not only is she a mom, but she is a "married single mom." Motherhood alone may not have swayed some of these women to stay home, but when combined with the other aspects of military life, many military spouses feel they have no real choice in the matter.

Questions for Reflection

If you are a parent yourself, use the following questions to reflect on your own situation. Pick one or two questions that are most relevant for your situation and take some time to answer them. Try writing out your answers in a private journal, or have a discussion with a friend or your spouse. Either way, be honest with yourself about where you are enjoying a good fit and where you could find room for improvement on this "M" of motherhood.

1. How has motherhood impacted your career? Is there anything you would do differently?
2. What is your personal definition of good mothering? How well are you living up to your own standards?
3. Whose opinion matters most to you about your parenting? What would they say about how well you are doing?
4. How well are you balancing working and parenting? What needs to change?
5. What support do you need to become a better mother? How will you get the support you need?
6. Do you and your spouse share the same viewpoints on parenting? Where do you differ?
7. If you are staying home, how satisfied are you in that role?
8. If you are working outside the home, how satisfied are you in that role?
9. How will your career goals change at different stages of your family life?

Chapter 4 – Military Life

Military life is the biggest factor that gets attention when we're talking about military spouse employment, and rightly so. The experience of military life can vary greatly depending on the service, career field, level of seniority, and location. But what many of us have in common is a life that demands the complete commitment of our life partners, to the point that they must be willing to give their very lives if called upon to do so. Although the dangers of military service are real, for most of us, the everyday impact of this lifestyle is not the stuff of action movies and life-or-death combat stories. It is the reality of living a life punctuated by periods of uncertainty, chaos, and disruption caused by relocation, deployments, and intense work demands.

Up until this point, the themes encountered in our stories could apply to just about any working wife or mother, military or civilian. Military spouses are no different from any working woman who has to navigate roles of wife and mother while maintaining a career. However, military life adds a third dimension that often creates serious obstacles for spouses who want to work.

In Chapter 1, we reviewed the sobering statistics on military spouse employment and the ways in which military life impacts earnings, unemployment, and underemployment. The stories in this chapter will bring life to some of those statistics, illustrating the complexities of military life and the myriad ways in which this lifestyle impedes full employment for spouses.

Employment issues experienced by military spouses most often stem from these common characteristics of military life: frequent relocation, service member work demands, and the limitations of overseas assignments. With most service members moving every 2 to 3 years, on average, frequent relocation poses serious problems for career-oriented spouses. Unless a spouse holds employment that is not tied to a specific location, each PCS requires a job change, very often leading to a discontinuous career path that stifles career progression and earnings (see Chapter 1). Relocation across state lines can also be a significant obstacle for spouses in career fields requiring state-specific licensing.

Service member work demands can include periods of absence due to deployments and TDYs, as well as intense or unpredictable schedules when the service member is home. Although these demands do not directly impact spouse employment, they create periods of time when the spouse must single-handedly run the entire household.

Overseas locations add a further complexity due to the limited employment opportunities available to military spouses. Most often, U.S. spouses are restricted to employment on the installation in foreign locations, due to work visa regulations and sometimes language barriers. With a captive labor pool vying for the same few jobs, competition for these positions is high. Furthermore, many available jobs are low-wage service and retail jobs that are not appealing to a skilled professional. Although any one of these issues could be surmountable, taken in totality, these obstacles imposed by military life often convince military spouses that working is not worth the effort it would require. This chapter includes several stories that describe how real-life spouses have wrestled with these challenges.

Roberta is one of several spouses in this chapter who are newlyweds coming to terms with the realities of military life. An experienced midwife, she is surprised to learn how difficult it is to continue her career, despite the fact that her family and friends seemed to already know this would be the case. She acknowledges there are some blessings to having a break from working, but says she struggles with feeling irrelevant.

Dee offers a youthful perspective of hope and gratitude, saying she never would be seeing the world and experiencing so many things if it were not for her marriage to a military man. Although she has had periods of loneliness and frustration as a new spouse so far from home, finding a job at the BX has given her a social outlet and purpose to her days. She is working on her degree, and hopes to become a Department of Defense Dependents Schools

(DoDDS)[12] teacher someday so she can have a more portable career that fits her new military life.

Charlotte is embarrassed to admit that she has become someone she used to look down upon, a "lady who lunches." An unemployed engineer, she is frustrated that she has been unable to find a job appropriate for her set of skills. She believes strongly that she should be putting her talent to good use, and feels guilty that she is not doing more, especially since she does not yet have children.

Phoebe is a former airman who separated from the Air Force in order to accompany her new husband and baby to Germany. Now, as a civilian spouse, she regrets her decision to leave the military and misses the sense of identity and security she felt as an active duty service member. She is struggling to find a place in military life now as a military spouse.

Maria began her marriage as an attorney with great hope for her continued career, but found her plans derailed by the need to take a new bar exam with each PCS. Although she successfully passed the first two bar exams and found gainful employment both times, she decided not to take a third bar exam when her health began to suffer during a pregnancy. She decided to put her health and child first and became a stay-at-home mom, a decision that made her feel like a failure until she learned to forgive herself.

---

[12] DoDDS schools are a network of primary and secondary schools that serve dependents of U.S. military and civilian DoD personnel assigned overseas.

Roberta

**"I wanted to have this life as a military spouse but
simultaneously have my career, which I still think is possible.
I just think it means changing certain concepts
around in my head."**

*Roberta had been a midwife for 10 years when she married her Air
Force husband. Unable to find work in Germany, she is enjoying a break
but is also feeling "irrelevant." She has been surprised that other spouses
don't ask about her career, and that her friends and family back home
expected her to stop working. As a new military spouse, she is just
beginning to make sense of her situation.*

It was definitely fulfilling to do birth and patient care, and to be
with women and families. But the hours were definitely long and
[I was] up a lot of nights. I think I spent more time complaining
about how tired I was than enjoying the job. But I can honestly say,
looking back on it now, that I enjoyed being a midwife. And I liked
the family and birth parts of it. I felt like midwifery is a profession,
not just an occupation. It's something I studied a long time for, and
at the 10-year mark, I felt like I was finally doing it, and feeling like
a professional midwife.

It felt like I was making a difference. I was using my [master's
in nursing] degree. I was finally at a point where half my loans were
paid off. So I wasn't struggling to just pay for my education, but
rather feeling like I was also making a good salary, and just feeling
like I was an accomplished single person. And then I was thinking
about how to apply that further, education wise, and so forth.

I'm a very goal-oriented person, and how I feel about myself as
a person is wrapped up in the accomplishments that I have made
through school and work. So when [my husband and I] met, I
definitely felt like my job was very important. If I were to put it on
a linear scale, I would say it was probably an 8 or a 9 out of 10, you
know, because it just sort of defined me. And, like I said, with

120

midwifery, people see you as that profession, instead of just your job.

Roberta was used to being defined by her professional role, and had to grapple with that loss when she and her new husband moved to Germany. As she describes it, however, it was a process that occurred over time because she could not fully understand this change in the beginning.

[At first] I think I was very excited about getting married and the process of us being together and moving. So that excitement overshadowed my ability to think through it. I don't think I had a concept of what it was really going to be like, to have to leave a job and say goodbye to people you've been working with for a long time. I can remember doing my last birth and thinking, "I don't know if I'm going to do this again. You know, this may never happen again." I was really sad when I had that moment, that realization.

I don't think I fully understood it, and then I had to start thinking, "Okay, where is my next job going to come from?" [Then] it occurred to me that my possibilities in that field would be limited. I'm limited to whatever military hospital we are near, if we are near one that has midwives. So, when that occurred to me, I thought, "Oh, I'll be okay. This will be rough but I think I can still do this." It wasn't until getting to Germany that I realized that it's quite a competitive process. It's one hospital with three midwives. They need a person or they don't. I think that was sort of a humbling experience. Until that point, I had pretty much gotten every job I had applied for. I wouldn't say things had been easy. It's always been hard work, but suddenly I was in a position where it just felt like you're not really that needed.

So, here was my sort of naïve thought: I thought I would take a month off in September, and then in October I would start looking, sending out resumes, getting online and going through the process, making contacts and finding other people that worked at the hospital, that sort of thing. So that's what I did, and it immediately began to be a very hard job hunt.

And then it's weird, once you realize how it's sort of a blessing to also be able to *not* have to work. To be presented with this opportunity to do other things, whether it's school or travel or have a baby, or those sorts of things. Once I realized that this was an amazing opportunity, I stopped being so stressed about it. I just sort of accepted that it's going to be hard to find a job. I would keep looking but I wouldn't be so stressed about it. So it's been 5 or 6 months. [There's] all this stuff I could have been doing and enjoying, [but] in the back of my mind, I'm constantly thinking, "I need a job right now, I need to pay my student loans, I need to do this..."

I feel like other people at home don't really understand because they say, "Well, yeah, you moved to Germany and now you're following [your husband] around the world. Isn't this what you thought it was going to be [like]?" Their idea of what they thought I should be thinking was totally different than what I was thinking. And then it occurred to me, "Wow, they totally got it." They knew that I would leave my job and now I'm with my husband and basically I'm on *his* career path. I didn't get that until people were reflecting this back to me.

After being forced to take a break from working, Roberta shifts her thinking and recognizes she has an unexpected opportunity. This realization lessens the stress of job searching, but still doesn't take away her need to feel valuable. She is shocked by the fact that her friends and family knew her career would be compromised, when she didn't really know this herself. Now she is trying to reconcile her need to "feel relevant" with her new life as a military spouse, and within her new environment in military circles.

It just felt like they weren't quite understanding my need to feel relevant. I wanted to feel like my job was still important, that my goals were still important, and I could do it. I wanted to have this life as a military spouse but simultaneously have my career, which I still think is possible. I just think it means changing certain concepts around in my head.

It was actually shocking to me when I first got [to Germany]. And this sounds terrible, because it makes it sound like I always need to be validated, or I need to have people ask about my job, which is not how I feel. I did immediately notice, [when] meeting with other spouses, people always asking, "What does your husband do? What does your husband fly?" Never, "What do *you* do?" And that's okay, but is it because the assumption is that I don't have [a job]? Or, is the assumption because I don't want to [work] or I'm not supposed to [work]? I don't know. I just felt sad. It just felt like I wasn't important, like I just didn't matter.

Like I said before, I don't think it's all bad, because I think it's an amazing opportunity to find other things you're interested in, a jumping-off point for education. Had I not done [all of] this, I probably would not be in a master's program in the fall. And, hopefully, when we leave here, I'll be prepared for the next career move, if it's in the states or wherever we go. I wouldn't have had that, had I not quit my job. So it can go either way.

I don't know if I can really pinpoint exactly what it was that made me have a change in mindset. I realized there were other things I could do. I just recently started [dog walking]. It's funny, my dad makes fun of me. I have a master's degree and I'm doing dog walking for people. I just decided to do other things with my time and also to feel like I'm contributing to the household. My husband doesn't have a problem with me not working, and we're fine on income, and there's no issue there. But I feel like I want to contribute to our household, or to pay my student loans, or whatever it is.

I feel like my self-esteem is such that I don't feel any depression about myself as a person. But I definitely feel a little bit lost, like there's no set structure to the day. I think I understand now what people say when they go into retirement, "Oh, I really looked forward to it." And then you get into it and you're a little isolated. I don't feel lesser of a person, but I definitely am experiencing emotions that I didn't have before when I had a job and a structured life.

Michelle Still Mehta

Roberta echoes the sentiments of several other spouses (Felice, Isabelle, Tanya, and Serena) who have talked about feeling at loose ends without the structure of a job to go to every day. In theory, she is willing to embrace this break from work and says it doesn't damage her self-esteem, but she still grapples with the daily challenge of finding purpose and meaning to her activities.

That lends to a feeling of a little bit of laziness. I think the more you isolate yourself, the more you tend to want to isolate. So if I'm having a day where I feel blah, I think I'm more inclined then to curl up and watch a movie on the Lifetime [channel]. Also, I feel sort of like a child that's been locked in the house all day. And then your spouse comes home and has a completely different emotion, which is, "I just got off of work and I want to sit here and do what you have been doing all day long." It's sort of this up-and-down roller coaster of emotion. Mostly, for me, it's coming from lack of structure, really wanting to contribute to our household and contribute to the world, and be relevant. As a person, you find other ways to do that. For instance, volunteering at a hospital – I'll be starting in a couple of months in that role. I never thought I'd do midwifery for free, but at least [I'd be] doing that same job. The salary, I've found, is not as important. I mean, it would be nice, like I said, to contribute to our household, but I need to be doing what I've been trained to do, what my vocation is. [I also need] to keep my brain stimulated and to have a structure. So, I'll be doing that and going to school. You find other ways to feel like you're continuing on the path you're supposed to be on.

The way I see it, it will probably be a rough 7 or 8 years if I am working as a midwife, because I'll be a new person wherever it is that we go to…You never get to gain a sense of seniority in one place.

You have to be flexible. You have to take what you get and mold it to what your goals are, and be able to bend them a little bit. To me, it means flexibility. It also means you have to be motivated too, which sometimes, given your circumstances in life, may not be easy. So, yeah, it means being flexible and motivated to find other

124

opportunities. If it's not something that's exactly what you want, look for something similar and be open to those opportunities that hopefully can lead to something good.

Roberta ends on a positive note, and advocates the need to be flexible as a military spouse. Like Heather (in Chapter 3), she never expected to volunteer her professional skills, but has decided it is worth doing for the sake of keeping up her skills and contributing. As an experienced midwife, she may be able to keep her career going, especially when they return stateside. In the meantime, it will be up to her to decide how to use this break she has been given.

Michelle Still Mehta

Dee

"It feels like I am making a contribution to my country in a small way."

Dee is a recent high school graduate, newly married to her Air Force husband. She feels lucky to have the opportunity to be in Europe and enjoys working at the BX so she can keep busy and have people to talk to. Dee is also in school, and would like to be a teacher someday. As a young adult at the very beginning of her military marriage, she is in the unique position of being able to speculate what her life and career will be like.

We were high school sweethearts and then he decided to enlist in the Air Force. It basically started from there. We graduated in May and he left in June. I went to see him graduate in August where he proposed to me.

Actually, the reason why we got married was a personal family situation. In August, I got kicked out of my house by my father and my husband felt bad for me, but it was a win-win situation. I wanted to get out of there. So when he came home for Christmas, we went to the courthouse and got married. Eventually, we're going to have a real wedding. I still have my dress. We got married in December, and then he left for Germany. I had to stay back because we had to get the sponsorship paperwork done [first].

I went to college for two semesters right after high school – summer and fall semester. And then I had to stop to get ready to come here [to Germany]. I had a part-time job at Dollar General for about a month and a half.

When he left, it was very stressful for me. I was living with his parents when he was in basic training. It was a really stressful environment because his mom was there and she had all those mixed feelings as a mom.

I also had no idea about the Air Force, and it was just totally new to me. My eyes were wide open for the whole entire time. It was an exciting time because of all the stuff that was happening and graduation too.

I wouldn't be in Germany [if it wasn't for the military]. A lot of people don't have those kinds of opportunities in life. That's what I think about all the time. It's exciting.

The first day he told me that I was going to be able to come here, I went to the post office and got my passport that day. I was really excited. I'd never been out of Ohio for my 19 years of living, so I was just really excited.

We had nothing, absolutely nothing, when we started out, so I was making lists and trying to get everything together. I was trying to go to garage sales to get everything we could. I mean we had nothing, so I was just trying to work to get all the money I could.

It was exciting [when I first got here] because I hadn't seen him in 6 months. [It was the] same thing with graduating from tech school and from basic training. You get used to not being able to see him. I [also] didn't have my driver's license at that time and I really had no idea what I was going to be doing. So, I was sitting at home with nothing to do for probably a good 3 or 4 months because I really didn't have anything to do. And I didn't have any friends yet.

I felt alone and I was really getting angry. Not really angry, but stressed out because I guess those were the couple of months that I was aggravated with him. And I was still trying to understand the Air Force. We had a couple of fights and I wasn't used to his schedule yet. His shop is open 24/7, so it's one of those rotating things. Sometimes you're on night shift. Sometimes you're on day shift. I really didn't get to see him that much. Obviously, in the Air Force, you don't. But I didn't know that at the time. I guess I was missing him.

Dee has faced her first test as a military spouse. She is excited to be overseas and is grateful for the opportunity to see a new part of the world, but also admits that she has had to adjust to some hard realities of military life. In the end, getting a job of her own helped her cope with her husband's unpredictable schedule, and kept her busy and socially active.

Right now, we're fine because I have a job and he has a job. We're getting along great. We pass each other sometimes, but it keeps you busy. You don't have to think about it that much.

I really wanted a job so I could help out and pay for bills. And he said, "Go ahead and do what you want." We have two cars now so we have to try to make that work with bills. I tried and tried for 3 months and then finally I was like, "I just need a job." So I went to the Base Exchange, and I really didn't care what kind of job I got. But I enjoy my job there. We make it work. Our days off are not on the same days at all, but I like it because it keeps us both busy. I don't have to sit at home anymore and think about all the things that are going on around me.

And then I started school in January. I'm feeling better about myself because I have a lot of things to do. I feel like I have a purpose because I'm pursuing a degree I've always wanted to pursue, and I'm able to contribute to our bills and everything.

I'm around people all the time. This is going to sound weird, but I was excited to get my job because I didn't really have anybody else to talk to, except for my husband. I was excited to get the job because I'd have people to talk to [at work]. I could talk to somebody about what's going on in my life instead of just keeping it all to myself, because I like to talk. I like to be around people. I [also] like to be around kids and I see kids on a daily basis, working in the infant's department. I enjoy it.

Looking ahead, Dee is optimistic about her future and the prospect of her husband staying in the Air Force. Her goal is to be a teacher, and she believes that teaching at a DoDDS school would be a good option for her if her husband chooses to stay in the military.

I would like to teach in an elementary school environment – kindergarten through fourth or fifth grade – but no higher than that, because little kids don't know anything when they come to school. You have the opportunity as a teacher to teach them something new, and they always have a smile on their face when they learn that piece of information. It's just exciting, seeing them learn.

We've talked about [what he wants to do]. We've only got as far as extending a year in Germany, so we really don't know where it's going to take us. He's talked about if he gets his school done in the time he's in the Air Force, then he might not [stay] in anymore. But that's up in the air right now.

I think it would be interesting if I could teach for a DoDDS school on base. If he continues in the military, that would be great. We'd have more opportunities to travel. That's one of the positive things in the Air Force – meeting new people that are in the same environment, I guess you could say.

People say on the news that Air Force wives have a very big impact on the country. I guess they're serving too, because they're living in a high-stress environment too. It feels like I am making a contribution to my country in a small way.

Dee is proud to be a new military spouse and likes the idea of serving her country alongside her husband. Although it is too soon to say how military life will impact her career, she seems to be looking at the future with eyes wide open, and is willing to forge a path where career and military life go hand in hand.

Michelle Still Mehta

Charlotte

"I want to work. I want to have that feeling that I accomplished something at the end of the day."

Charlotte has been a military spouse for 3 years, and recently moved to Germany for her first military move. With a background in civil engineering, she has not yet been able to find work in her field, and has been working as a substitute teacher on base at the DoDDS school. She feels guilty for not working full time and is chagrined to find herself becoming one of the military spouses she used to look down upon. She wonders what the future will hold for her as her husband continues to progress in his military career, and they consider starting a family.

I never, ever thought I would do anything but get a job. In my family, my mom works and my dad's a farmer, so I always worked when I was growing up. I have always had jobs ever since high school, through college and everything. Now I kind of feel like I'm a bump on a log because I don't have any children yet either. I should be making money and saving up for the future. I don't want to be vain or anything, but I made good grades in school, and I felt like I was a smart enough person that I should be working. I should be using my brain rather than feeling like it's atrophying. I just want to work.

[Working gives me that] satisfaction that you have something to do with your day. The projects that we did [at my engineering firm in Georgia] were good. My boss was involved in financial-aid type stuff and rehabilitation projects. I feel like we actually did good for the community because we would help them get government grants and loans for low-to-moderate income areas. There was some satisfaction in seeing [improvement in] a neighborhood that was kind of lower end, flooded all the time, or [where] you could smell their sewer. A project might take a while but, eventually, they had this nicer area and then their property value probably went up. There was that feeling of satisfaction. It

130

was just a feeling that you had something that you're doing with your life. I want to work. I want to have that feeling that I accomplished something at the end of the day.

But we said we wanted to go to Europe. We're young, we don't have children. We *love* traveling. And my husband said, "You know, it will be hard to get a job." I said, "Okay, whatever." I've never, ever *not* gotten a job that I applied for, until here. So I thought, "We're going to live in Europe. I don't care." So we put Germany as our number one [assignment choice]. And then, by this time, my bosses knew that I was going to be moving. I was with my coworker on the road doing a project when my husband called. And I just said, "Ahhh! I'm moving to Germany." I was thrilled to be [coming] here. I love being here... and now I can't find a job.

It's not working out like I thought it would. I've been applying, and, in the meantime, I got a substitute teaching job because it would give me a little bit of money and just keep me doing something during the day. Then we found out my husband was going to deploy, so I thought, "Oh, my God! What am I going to do on a deployment?"

Charlotte was initially confident that finding employment would not be a big deal, but after more than a year in Germany, she is frustrated that her plans have not yet come to fruition. She does not regret coming to Germany, but now realizes how much time and energy it can take to find employment with an overseas move.

I got a call the other day about an energy engineer [position]. And I thought, "Oh, this will be cool. I could do that." I had gotten the email that said, "We're referring you to the hiring official." That happens all the time, and then they send me another email that says, "We didn't pick you." [But] I got a call. And I was all excited. But then he called to ask what my DEROS date was. Everyone says they're not supposed to ask you that. And I thought, "Well, what am I going to do, tell them they're not supposed to ask me that?" I kind of have to answer the question. So I told him, and we've [already] been here a year and a couple months now. So, are they going to say, "Well, we're not even going to look at her because she's out of time?" Now I'm wondering, should I even try anymore because I'm only going to have another year and a half here? Do I give up? I don't know.

[Maybe I should] just apply for anything to stay busy – secretary, whatever. But I've gotten to the point where I think, "You know what? Forget those things." We've only got a year and a half left [in Germany], and if it's not going to be professional, or in my degree program, or what I studied, or put me toward getting that Professional Engineer [PE] license, then I'm not going to try anymore. So I'm just focusing on that. I'm at a place right now where it may not happen. I might just have to accept it and quit complaining that I get to travel and have fun all day.

Charlotte says she may just have to accept her unemployed status and be content. She didn't expect to find herself in this situation, so now she must wrestle with the emotions and self-judgment she is faced with as a result. She also seems to question whether this break from work is a temporary setback or a long-term change in her role and identity.

I still kind of cry to my husband every once in a while, "I'm stupid. Nobody thinks I'm smart. I can't get a job." And he says, "It's not that; it's Europe." I'll talk to someone and they'll say, "I can't get a job either." And I'll think, "Well, you're really smart. I don't see why you couldn't get one." Then I feel better. It's kind of a roller-coaster ride. I'm just really worried that I'll go back to the U.S. and [then] are they going to think that I wasn't smart enough to get a job or qualified enough? Or are they going to think I was lazy by taking a 3-year break? Are they going to think I'm behind other people my age who have their PE by now?

We've talked about when we get back to the U.S. and probably starting a family. And I know they can't *not* hire you, but, in my last job, we did some outdoor stuff. I had to go climb down manholes and stuff like that. I'm afraid that I'll get a job, then I'll get pregnant, and they'll be like, "Thanks a lot!" So, I'm wondering if this is it. Was my 3 years [back] in Georgia going to be my whole career? Am I never going to find a job again? Was I on a roll and then did it end? Am I just going to be a mom now – which is not bad, but, in

132

my mind, I always thought I'd be a working mom because my mom was.

I guess the attitude in my house growing up was [looking down on] the ladies who lunch. My mom would always say, "Oh, the tennis girls..." because she's still at work. She probably was a little jealous because she had sisters or friends whose husbands made a good enough salary where they didn't have to work, and could be full-time moms, and they were happy. But my dad was a farmer and my parents couldn't afford it. My parents sent us to private school and they made a lot of sacrifices. My mom is in her 50s. She still works and I don't. I'm her daughter. I'm a lady who lunches now. So there's a little bit of me feeling like I need to tell my mom, "I promise, I'm still looking for a job. I don't want you to feel disappointed in me." It's just how I was raised. You work.

Like several other spouses we have heard from (e.g., Grace, Maria, and Felice), Charlotte uses her own mother as both a role model and a reason for finding herself falling short. If her own mother was still working, how could she possibly justify not doing the same? This seems to only add to her sense of guilt and wavering confidence.

I'm not as confident [now] because I feel like maybe they're not picking me because I'm not smart or qualified enough. And then I'm wondering if I'm forgetting stuff. Sometimes I'll be in the grocery store and I'm trying to add up something. I'll think, "Oh, God, I can't do basic math in my head!" I feel like I'm not using that part of my brain as much. I wonder, am I getting – not dumber – but am I just getting out of that mindset? And will I get back into it if I get a job again, or would I be behind other people?

I think you have to have something to show for your life. I just feel like God put us here to work. I feel bad. There's people out there who don't have what I have. I feel like I'm undeserving of everything that I have if I don't work for it. I feel bad that I have all of these things, and this wonderful life, and I don't even have to work for it now. Other people would love to have this and they work hard.

Michelle Still Mehta

What's life about if it's not working or helping others? If I had children, maybe that [is] helping someone else. You're accomplishing something. You're raising a new person. That would be satisfying. But what am I accomplishing by not working? I don't feel like I should be able to just do whatever I want just because my husband makes a good enough salary that I don't have to work.

As Charlotte tries to make sense of her situation and the emotions she is feeling, the prospect of starting a family adds to the uncertainty of her future career plans. Ultimately, she is unable to answer all the questions she is holding, but trusts that God will guide her on the right path.

I feel up and down lately because I've been thinking [that] I don't want children for a while. I want to put it off, but some of our friends are starting to have children. And I told my husband, "You need to just pray for me to have a change of heart about children because I don't know how I feel about them." So, in the last couple of months, he must be praying for me. [Now] I think, "Well, okay, it'd be kind of cool to be a mom." So now there's this factor on the side where I wonder, "Hmm. Would I work? Would I work full time? Could I get a part-time thing? Could I do that?" I don't know. I feel like my hopes and dreams are a little bit in flux now because I don't know what I want to do anymore. It's really fuzzy.

I think God will put his will in my life, and if he has a job for me, then I guess it'll happen. So maybe I haven't gotten a job yet because of other reasons. Maybe I had to learn some stuff about myself and make these friends so that I might be more open to being a mom later. I don't know how I feel. But I have to think about it so much more than I ever used to, which is kind of annoying. Because I had a job, I was good, I was be-bopping along and now it's like, "What do I want to be? What do I want to do? What can I do? Maybe I'll apply for this job. Maybe I'll do this later." I don't know. I don't feel like I'm really a grown-up yet because I don't know what's going to happen.

Charlotte recognizes that her life is in transition, and acknowledges that she does not have all the answers. A big part of this transition has

134

included a shift from being outside the military to being inside the military. She used to keep herself distant from the other military spouses she looked down upon, but now realizes what it is like to be one of those spouses and is humbled by the realization. Whether temporary or not, this period of unemployment has given her a new appreciation for the experiences of others, and has taught her an important lesson about not judging other people.

I had no idea what I was getting myself into. I don't think my husband did either. Whenever we were in [Georgia], my husband was in the Air Force and I worked there. That was how it was and I wasn't involved in any of the on-base stuff. It wasn't ever a really big factor. I hadn't shopped on base. I didn't do my grocery shopping there. I didn't go to the doctor on base. So it wasn't really a major factor except that we lived in Georgia instead of in Louisiana, near our families. And since we've gotten here [Germany], it's just so much more. I'm on the base every day. I shop there. I go to the doctor there, go to the library there. The way I've made friends is through spouse clubs [there]. So all of a sudden, I'm this "Air Force wife," when before, I *was*, but it didn't really matter then. It was just my husband's job.

I feel like I'm more defined by my husband because he's the breadwinner, and he's the one with the job. It's his career that we're following, and I'm here for him, which is kind of annoying, [but] it's not a big deal. I feel like saying, "I had my own thing before."

Sometimes I'm a little snooty. "I'm not like y'all. I'm not *just* a spouse. I have my own thing." I don't need to be defined by my husband because a lot of people are. [I know that sounds] rude, but I think that you need to work. You need to have a goal. You need to be in school. You need to be doing something. And if you're not, and you're just what I am… I'm kind of something I didn't want to be. I'm just a spouse now, because I don't really have a daily purpose.

I've also come to the conclusion that these women who are like me are not just mooches, or they're not out getting their nails done every 5 minutes, like I had in my mind when I worked. [I used to

135

think] "How are these girls getting their nails done at 10:00 a.m. and chilling at Target?" Some of them were probably like me. They want to work, or they work and I don't know it. I've learned that I'm not a nice person for thinking that way about people. It makes me [see that] everybody has their own thing, and what works for me probably doesn't work for another person.

I hope that I will get a GS position here. Everyone says [that] once you're in the system, you can transfer. So I'll just try to go back to my old-school way of living and I'll get a job. But now I know that there are resources at the base and ways to make friends. I'll try to be a little more involved. I think it's probably almost a good thing that this has happened to me, because if I can learn something from it, I'll be a more rounded person rather than [feeling] like work is everything.

Charlotte's closing comment is a telling example of what many military spouses experience in their career struggles. Through involuntary experiences of unemployment or underemployment, we often learn that there is more to life than our careers, and work is not everything. Although we may dislike the disruptive aspects of military life, there is also an intangible silver lining. We grow in ways that other working professionals may not, simply because we are forced to let go of those professional lives from time to time, and are forced to develop other parts of ourselves. Like many other military spouses, Charlotte must ask herself, "Who would I be if I weren't an engineer?" Whether we like it or not, military life often challenges our core identities, while also giving us the unique opportunity to discover new aspects of who we are. For those spouses who are comfortable exploring these new possibilities, military life can be an exciting and healthy experience. For those who cling tightly to a singular definition of themselves, the constant need to adapt may be a painful struggle.

Phoebe

"[Being in] the Air Force was awesome...But in this civilian life, there are no rules. There are no expectations. There are no guidelines. People can hurt you and just walk away and it's okay."

Phoebe is an Air Force veteran and spent several years on active duty as a professional photographer. During her years in the military, she was a single mom, and she fondly recalls how fulfilled she felt during this period of her life. Since then, she has gotten married, separated from the military, and had a second child. Now she is unsatisfied with her life circumstances and is struggling with feelings of depression. Although she had no desire to leave the military when she did, she felt she had no other choice when she learned she was pregnant and the Air Force denied requests from her and her new husband to be stationed together in the same location.

I was hoping to get the 20 years for retirement. I didn't want to get out. I loved the camaraderie, the feeling that you get when you're around other people. I liked the service to your country that you do and how much people respect you for putting your life on the line. I didn't even feel like it was a job because I wanted to do it. I melted into the military really well. And I like it a lot. I did. I still do. It was everything about me.

Even when it was the worst day ever, I still loved my job. I felt very comfortable putting on the uniform. I felt very comfortable with finances. I was really good at that. I felt even more comfortable being in the Air Force. I felt more comfortable as a mom because I have more patience. I had all the patience in the world and I had the power to stick up for myself. I had the staff sergeant rank coming to me that I worked hard for. It satisfied me so much as a person, I didn't need anything else. My work was enough. And then, when I came home, I had all the patience left in the world for my child. When I came home, even though I was exhausted from

137

work sometimes, I would get a second, third, fourth, fifth wind after coming home. However exhausting the day was, it didn't matter.

When I was first stationed at Ramstein, I was a photojournalist. And that's where all the traveling came in. I got to go TDY with the U.S. Air Forces in Europe Band to the Ukraine and Romania, and saw how they influenced other cultures, other people, other countries, and that was really awesome.

Then I moved to Wilford Hall [Ambulatory Surgical Center in San Antonio, Texas]. Since that's a research hospital, I was [a medical photographer]. The worst part was the suicides, [taking pictures of] the autopsies. I also did preop and postop [photos] for surgeries, and a lot of women would come in. This one woman, the first one I ever did, she came in diagnosed with breast cancer hours before. And when she came in for the photos, she just looked at me with these eyes, like, "Do I have to do this?" Women don't want to strip down and take pictures when we already feel vulnerable from being diagnosed with breast cancer. But I had to tell her, "Yes, you do, because having these photos makes it easier for the doctor to reconstruct [the breasts later on]." I think I've seen almost every shape of woman there is possible because of the studio. And then, being a woman, I was the only female there in the shop. The majority of our people coming in were female, so I did them all. It was rewarding, too, because people started to get to know me and feel comfortable [with me]. But as soon as I started getting comfortable in my title as medical photographer, I had to pick up and leave – not only leave San Antonio, but leave the Air Force – and that was rough.

Phoebe explains the series of events that led to her separation from the Air Force. When she moved from Ramstein to San Antonio, she left a boyfriend behind in Germany who was also active duty Air Force. She says her boyfriend proposed to her the night before she left Germany, much too late to change her assignment plans. Shortly after arriving in San Antonio, she also learned she was pregnant. At that point, Phoebe and her boyfriend decided to get married in order to increase their chances of being stationed together, but their plans did not work out the way they had hoped. Phoebe's new husband put in for an assignment to nearby Lackland Air Force Base, also in San Antonio, and submitted documentation from Phoebe's physician supporting the move, only to have the request denied by his superior.

We just had to get married on a whim because that's the only way the Air Force was going to move us. It's like playing chess. You have to sacrifice one thing. I didn't want to get married right away, not that quickly. I didn't care about my parents hounding me for having a child out of wedlock. Screw my parents because they're way too formal. I just didn't want to jump into marriage because I felt the military was forcing me to [get married] again. And I just wasn't comfortable. At the same time, you do what you have to do. So I did the marriage thing and got the paperwork going. I even had my doctor write a letter saying that it would be for my benefit health wise for him to be stationed in San Antonio because I was at high risk of losing the baby. I was still passing blood, even 6 months along. And the stress really wasn't helping. We ended up getting married by proxy while I was in Airman Leadership School, which was interesting. He wasn't even there.

Then the command chief for the training side of Lackland opened up a job slot for my husband. All we needed was his DEROS curtailed.[13] So I have all this ammo, that's what it felt like. All these letters of recommendation by people, letters saying it would be better if he was there, lots of leadership on my husband's side was pushing for it too. And they actually approved the DEROS curtailment at first. But then his chief erased it and checked, "No." It was approved by the colonel and the chief said, "No, Colonel, I don't think that this should be approved. We shouldn't be curtailing a DEROS for this reason." That same chief even emailed my doctor saying, "How dare you write this letter and present us

---

[13] A DEROS curtailment would allow a service member to return from an overseas assignment earlier than planned.

with this?" I felt like crap, like I was going to beat the crap out of that chief.

I got out, based on the pregnancy, because that was the only option. I really cut it close. I was due April 4 and I put in the paperwork only 2 months before I was due. I only felt comfortable with it because they said I could go into the inactive reserve.

After separating from the military, Phoebe returned to Germany to be with her new husband. Now there with an infant and a 3-year-old, she is a stay-at-home mom and a student, and is struggling with the loss of her Air Force career.

I started going to school here [in Germany] and I get paid $2,000 a month to go to school full time, so that's kind of nice. But it's just not the same. It's not the same satisfaction as being in the Air Force. I was doing a service to my country and I was always proud. I was so proud of my dad [who was also in the Air Force] every time he came home. And I loved the uniform. People think I'm silly because, when I was in basic training, I put on the uniform and I just did a little dance. I thought, "I have my own!" I used to wear my dad's uniform and pretend that it was mine and now I had my own. My dad and I developed this really strong bond too. I'd say, "Did you get your uniform? I went and bought mine! Did you go get your stripes? I bought mine!" He was going to come and tack on my staff sergeant stripes for me [if I had not separated]. He was going to be in his blues [service dress].

Phoebe goes on to describe what she was thinking when she decided to separate from the Air Force. She thought that becoming a student and stay-at-home mom would be an acceptable substitute for her Air Force career, but she has not been happy about her transition to civilian life.

[I thought I would] go to school. I always had that in my head, not realizing that being a stay-at-home mom [means] you don't have time for anybody or anything else except for [your kids]. It was hard to get all that school work done. When am I going to get it all done?

And when you move to a new place, you don't develop a support network overnight. I tried to get involved in the spouses' club. That's a big, gossip spider web of women. I'll tell you that much. I'm sure some spouses' organizations are great, but this one is not. It doesn't fit me. The Air Force fit me. Not the spouses' "gab-gab" session. That just doesn't suit me very well. And all these people would say, "Oh, I'll help you, but you live too far away." Okay, then don't tell me you're going to help me, especially when I call on you and I need it. It's just so hard dealing with this.

Stay-at-home moms always seem so happy and great, but when you get in their cliques, they're mean. They're so mean and then they suck the life out of you. At least that's what it felt like for me. [Being in] the Air Force was awesome. At least I knew what to expect from the Air Force and I was okay with that. There were rules. There were guidelines so you know exactly what's going to happen if you mess up, because it's written right out there. But in this civilian life, there are no rules. There are no expectations. There are no guidelines. People can hurt you and just walk away and it's okay.

Phoebe feels a huge void now without her Air Force identity. She misses the structure, the routine, the sense of purpose that she felt, even the uniform. She says the Air Force was "everything" about her, and now she is forced to reinvent a new identity for herself as military spouse and mother. This transition has been hard for her, and she finds herself struggling with feelings of depression, an issue she has battled with her whole life. (Note: Resources were discussed with Phoebe after this interview took place, and she acknowledged that she was receiving counseling from a mental health professional to help with her depression.)

Little things started to affect me tenfold, more than they normally would have. I started paying attention to things. I realized that I had feelings of not wanting to live anymore. Every morning I'd wake up and I didn't want to be here. I just didn't want to do anything. I didn't want to run a marathon anymore. I feel more exhausted now being a stay-at-home mom than I ever did being a single mom, working and pregnant. How is that possible? I wonder if it has something to do with the way I'm thinking, more of a mind-over-matter type of thing. I think my brain is just messing me up with my new life.

It's not fitting [me] like I thought it would. [Staying home] is not as rewarding as I hoped it would be. And it's very selfish, I think, to say that. I feel guilty saying it. But it's really not as rewarding. I need a break and I don't get a break anymore. Or, they are very few and far between. Little things get me down and depressed very easily. I don't feel the same satisfaction I felt from being in the Air Force.

As an outsider, it is easy to understand why Phoebe may feel unhappy and depressed. By giving up a part of herself that defined her in such an important way, there is an emptiness she does not yet know how to replace. The role the military offered her provided purpose and reassurance that she was doing something that mattered. Although she expected to feel good about staying home with her children, she is not finding the same sense of reward and purpose. Whether she finds an answer through the military or an alternative career path, Phoebe will need to find a new role that gives her satisfaction and meaning.

Maria

"Every time you PCS, your life is in pieces and you have to start all over again."

Maria was an ambitious and successful attorney determined to keep her career going through every PCS, which meant passing the bar exam in each state she moved to.[14] After working hard to keep up her credentials with each move, she reluctantly chose not to sit for the bar exam in a third new state. Ultimately, she says she had to forgive herself and move on, but she remains critical of the military for creating real obstacles for professional military spouses.

I was a domestic violence prosecutor in Puerto Rico, and I had a lot of prestige because I was a prosecutor. I was very lucky that they were looking for recent graduates from law school with the bar to hire them and make them prosecutors. That was a once-in-a-lifetime opportunity. That gave me so much prestige that law students who knew me said, "I want what you have. When I graduate, I want to be just like you." That gives you an example of how lucky and what a good position I had. I was only 25 years old and police officers were calling me "Honorable Prosecutor." It was scary, too, because I had a lot of power. I could send people to jail. But wow, I was so proud of myself. I was very proud of myself. I thought, "Wow, I did it!"

But I was in love, and my husband was an American military guy, so I had to leave everything behind – my family, my friends, my career – and move to Biloxi, Mississippi. It was a sweet and sour experience because I was a newlywed. I was so much in love. But it

---

[14] The practice of law is one of many professions that requires state-specific licensing, making relocation especially difficult for military spouses in those fields. Nursing and teaching are two other common professions that require licensing. Although some states have enacted legislation to accommodate military spouses and accept licenses from out of state, this issue is still a barrier for many military spouses in a variety of professions.

was tough leaving everything behind. And I had to focus on perfecting my English, so I started taking English classes on base. It was stressful.

It was a tough decision. All my family were saying, "Are you sure about this? You're going to get married and leave everything behind?" But I was in love. And I said, "You know what, I'll find another job. I'll pass the bar in the United States. I'll do whatever it takes. This doesn't mean the end of my career." Or, so I thought...

Maria contrasts her initial euphoria of falling in love and getting married with the realities of what military life turned out to be. Although her family had concerns about the challenges ahead for her, she didn't appreciate how difficult her career challenges would be until she experienced them for herself.

I didn't understand what it means to be a military wife at all. I didn't understand that I had to move all the time. The first couple of months, as a newlywed, everything was like an adventure, but it was very difficult for me to accept the fact that I had to depend on my husband. [Before] I was making my own money and I was buying fancy clothing or nice stuff because I could afford it. And now I felt so guilty that I had to use my husband's money.

My mom worked all her life so my example was [that of] a working mother. My mom has her own business, a very powerful lady. So I felt like, "What's wrong with me? I live off of my husband." I was focusing on perfecting my English and being [fully] bilingual because I wanted to go back to work as soon as possible. I was afraid I was going to be discriminated against with a Puerto Rican diploma. So I went back to school for my LLM [Master of Laws degree] in health law.[15]

Then we moved to Florida. It was a lot of sacrifice once again, but I passed my bar [exam] the first time. I was very proud of myself. A lot of people didn't pass the bar and English is their first

---

[15] Maria is hoping that earning this additional credential of an LLM degree will improve her chances of being admitted to the bar and landing employment.

language, and I was able to pass the bar and I did very well. My dad was so proud of me.

I tried to find a job in my line of work, in health law. I kept applying and I couldn't find a job. After months and months, I found a job in a field that I never even considered, in insurance defense. But I didn't like it because insurance defense has nothing to do with family or people. I wasn't enjoying my job. I was miserable.

And my husband said, "This is not worth it." I was working 7 days a week. So I quit. My husband supported me 100%. But it was tough because I was making my own money again.

[I decided] I'm going to go back to my roots. I'm going to go back to family law and domestic violence because I think that's my calling. I started working as a volunteer [for a legal services agency]. And, very quickly, they were very happy with me. The first time they had a paying job [for me], it was a temporary attorney job, substituting for this lady that needed breast cancer surgery. She trained me and I did her job; it was helping people represent themselves in court. It was with the public coming [in as] walk-ins, and I loved it. It was a very good job. And they were very pleased with me.

Right after that, they had an opening for a family law attorney...yes! And they wanted a bilingual person. The problem was my husband had to PCS. We were hoping to stay in Florida. Unfortunately, it didn't work out, so we had to go to San Antonio [Texas]. That was bad news. I cried so much. I was devastated because I was so happy with my job.

They said, "It's too bad you have to leave, but we don't care. You give us whatever time you can give us and we'll have you. And then, when you're leaving, we'll put out an advertisement to look for somebody else." So I loved it. I was so happy. I would be singing in the morning going to work. It's so hard for a person to find a job that you look forward to every morning.

Now with two assignments under her belt, Maria feels like military life is derailing her career. Although she has been persistent and tenacious,

145

she has still endured a roller coaster of both accomplishments and losses. After completing her LLM, passing a second bar exam in Florida, and leaving a law firm job that made her miserable, she finally found a job that was a perfect fit for her. For that reason, the news about her next PCS to San Antonio was particularly devastating.

When it was time to say goodbye, I cried a lot. When I arrived in San Antonio, I was so depressed. I stayed a whole week in bed. I didn't want to get out. I said, "No, I don't want to go anywhere. I don't want to see San Antonio. I don't want to be here." I felt bad for my husband, but it really hurt me so much leaving my job. I had to say goodbye and start all over again.

Every time you PCS, your life is in pieces and you have to start all over again. It is very hard to be a military wife. People don't understand that, but it's a lot of sacrifice. That's why, when you see people criticizing benefits to military people, I say, "They don't understand. This is a lot of sacrifice. It's not only the soldiers but also the families." Oh, my God, I'm sorry...

Maria begins to cry...

I felt so miserable. I wanted to be an attorney, but I [had not taken] the bar exam [in Texas] so I couldn't work as an attorney [there]. I decided to take the bar for the third time. Then I found out I was pregnant. It was a very tough pregnancy. Two weeks before the bar, I started getting very, very, very sick. I started having contractions. And I feared that I was going to lose my baby. So something told me inside, "If you keep pushing yourself, and if you keep doing this, you're going to lose your baby. You're harming your baby with all this stress." So I told my husband, "I'm not going to do this." So I postponed [the bar exam]. I said, "I'm not going to take the bar. I'm dedicating myself to my baby."

But it was hard. I got depressed. I felt like I failed. I felt like I couldn't do it. It was important for me to have another bar because I thought, "Oh, I will feel prestigious!" I got really depressed, to the point that I was in bed crying. And my mom said, "You have to forgive yourself for not doing this or you're going to harm your baby, you're crying so much." But I felt defeated. It took me a while to accept that I didn't do it. I couldn't do it. But it's okay. I'm a human.

I felt like a school dropout. I was ashamed of myself. And you always have the fear that if you take a pause in your career, then nobody will want to hire you. I set myself a goal and I didn't do it. I had never dealt with failure before in my life, never. I've always been so successful. I was also worried about other people's opinion. I know it's silly, but they're going to think less of me because I didn't do the bar.

Maria reached her breaking point in San Antonio. If not for her health, she may have pushed through it and taken this bar exam. The experience of a difficult pregnancy, however, on top of a third move and third bar exam was too stressful for her to endure. Not only did she have to accept what this meant for her employment prospects, but she also had to reconsider her very identity. Suddenly, she was no longer defined as a hard-driving professional, but was rather identified as a stay-at-home mom, a role she never thought she would play.

It took me a while to accept [my situation], because I never thought of myself as a stay-at-home mom. I always looked at myself as a professional. Every time I saw a lady with children, staying at home, "No. That's not going to be me. I'm going to be the professional." It was hard to accept my fate that I'm going to be a stay-at-home mom. It was hard. It took almost 2 months to forgive myself and not feel guilty anymore.

All my memories are of my mom working and being dressed up to go to work, with her makeup and her high heels. I always looked at her and admired her so much. That was the kind of example that I had. That's my role model: my mother. And that's what I wanted to be.

At this point, Maria's daughter is in preschool and she has accepted her role as a full-time mother for the time being. However, she still laments the sacrifice she has had to make, feeling she has been forced to give up her career in order to be a military spouse.

Maybe it's silly of me for thinking like this, but sometimes I'm afraid. My husband has such a very nice, prestigious job. He does something really, extremely important, saving people's lives every day. He can come home and talk about work and he feels so good about himself. I can see it in his eyes, that passion. He loves his job. He loves it and I cannot share. I don't have any input. Sometimes I'm afraid my husband is not going to find me interesting anymore. What do I have? What can I talk about – what I saw on TV or what I talk about with the girls out for coffee?

I never thought it was going to be this hard, to the point that I tell girls, "Oh, are you dating a military guy? End it now before you fall in love." I'm sorry, but, as I said, it's hard. If you really love your job and your career, you have to think twice. You have to sacrifice a lot for love, for the love of your husband. You have to sacrifice practically *who* you are.

Maria's closing remarks speak volumes about the true impact of military spouse employment challenges. The sacrifice is not only about income or career advancement, but is central to who we are as human beings. For military spouses who have worked hard to create a professional identity, giving up that identity feels like giving up an important piece of who you are.

Lessons on Military Life

The stories from this chapter reveal some of the challenges military life can pose, as well as some of the hidden blessings. Whether a newlywed, seasoned spouse, or former service member, each of these women has learned to navigate the complexities of military life. Here are a few lessons I take away from these stories:

1. **Overseas assignments are a mixed blessing.** Charlotte and Roberta both speak about how hard it has been to find employment in Germany. They were both optimistic about their prospects, knowing they had never had problems finding employment in the past, and didn't fully appreciate how limited employment opportunities would be at an overseas military installation. At the same time, they both acknowledge that there have been some upsides to living overseas as a military spouse. Charlotte explains that she was thrilled to come to Germany for the travel opportunities; and Roberta admits that it has been a blessing to have the freedom to do things other than work. Dee readily shares that she feels very fortunate to live in a foreign country, an opportunity she never would have had otherwise. These stories exemplify the mixed blessings of overseas assignments and one of the central realities of military life – moving to new and exciting locations is both an adventure and a burden. Grappling with that tension is a necessary part of being a military spouse.

2. **New military spouses experience a transition period where they have to make sense of their new reality.** Many of the women in these stories expressed the fact that they thought they knew what to expect but really didn't fully know what military life would be like until they experienced it. This is a normal psychological process of sense making that anyone encounters during a major life

change. We have initial expectations about the future, and then must wrestle with reconciling the gap between those expectations and reality once this anticipated change becomes our lived experience. Sometimes we protect ourselves from the negative aspects of a change by allowing ourselves to ignore painful truths that are obvious to others. Roberta discusses this quite poignantly when she says her family and friends all understood that her career would probably be put on hold somewhat when she got married and moved to Germany. Roberta found this out to be true, but really had no such expectation when she first got married. Now that she sees what being a military spouse is like, she explains that she is playing with concepts in her head to find a way to keep her career going. During this transition period, she is having an internal negotiation to make sense of her situation. Can I actually keep my career? What would it take? Why is this so challenging? All military spouses experience this transition period in one way or another, whether it is dramatic or not. We all have to reconcile our new reality with what we thought military life would be like, and make sense of what this means for us.

3. **Frequent relocation is a significant obstacle to military spouse careers.** As the stories in this book illustrate, military spouses face a myriad of employment challenges and finding career success requires a strategy that will fit all aspects of one's life. However, if I had to pick one single barrier to spouse employment that looms above all others, it would certainly be the challenge of frequent relocation. Deployments and unpredictable schedules can make it difficult for spouses to work, but those problems are potentially solvable with better access to childcare. Frequent relocation is harder to remedy, forcing spouses to choose between reinvention with each new PCS or not working at all. The result is often a career with lower wages

and less advancement than one would otherwise attain, or simply no career at all.

Maria's story is a heartbreaking example of the devastating effects of frequent relocation. As a lawyer, she found it especially challenging to PCS between states and be forced to take a new bar exam each time if she wanted to maintain her career. Her tenacity is impressive, but even she reaches a breaking point where facing another bar exam and job search on top of a difficult pregnancy was too much. I expect that Maria has the ability to return to her law career when she is ready, but her story demonstrates the frustration that so many military spouses experience. Sometimes the continuous moving around just becomes too much, especially when combined with parenting and other demands. The effort seems futile, at least temporarily so, especially in career fields that require state-specific licensing. For many spouses who do forge successful career paths, finding a way to break the cycle of professional reinvention with each move is essential. Many do so by choosing a career that is portable and sustainable throughout geographic moves.

4. **Military life can have a significant impact on one's identity and sense of self.** Phoebe is struggling to make sense of her new reality as a military spouse instead of a military service member. She wonders how she can be so much more exhausted now as a spouse and stay-at-home mom than she was as a full-time service member. She acknowledges her battle with depression, but is looking for a way to accept the loss she is feeling after leaving the Air Force. She doesn't feel like she fits in as a civilian spouse, and is trying to forge a new identity for herself that does fit. Although Phoebe's case may be an extreme one, we all have to come to terms with our military spouse identity in some

151

way. We have to acknowledge how military life has changed us, how it may impact us going forward, and how we want to tackle what lies ahead. The key here is to be open to change without becoming lost – to make healthy accommodations for military life without sacrificing who we are at the core.

Questions for Reflection

Here is another opportunity for you to reflect on your own situation and evaluate your own military life. Review the following list of questions and pick one or two to explore in depth. Write your answers in a personal journal or discuss them with a friend or your spouse. How well does the "M" of military life fit for you?

1. How has military life impacted your career?
2. Do you and your spouse have a common understanding about his/her future in the military and how long he/she plans to stay in? If not, why not?
3. In what ways has military life been positive for you?
4. When you think about the future, what worries do you have about your military life?
5. How have PCS moves and other aspects of military life impacted your career so far?
6. What can you do to minimize the impact of these challenges?
7. Who do you know that seems to thrive as a military spouse? How could you be more like him/her?
8. What are your career plans during military life? How do you expect them to change after military life?
9. What positive or negative aspects of military life have been surprising or unexpected to you? What would you change if you had understood these realities from the beginning?
10. What aspects of yourself and your identity are most precious to you? What are you not willing to compromise or change?

Chapter 5 – Integrating the 3 Ms

The stories in this chapter highlight spouses who have found a way to integrate their careers into three important aspects of their lives: marriage, motherhood, and military life. Like the rest of the stories, these are not picture-perfect lives without struggle, but lives of women who have found a path that works for them. They express gratitude and satisfaction with their current situation, and acknowledge sacrifices they have made along the way to find the spot that is just right for them. These women are also mindful about their priorities and they make decisions about what matters most to them at a given period of their lives. They have accepted the need to compromise, but are unwilling to sacrifice their commitments to their families or their dreams as individuals.

Vanessa is a self-employed photographer who started out as a stay-at-home mom. After a career in early childhood intervention, she was confident in her decision to stay home with her children during their preschool years. Although she was happy as a mother, she realized she needed something for herself as well and discovered a love for photography. Her decision to start her own business has served her well with a mobile military lifestyle, and has given her an anchor in her life, especially during her husband's multiple deployments.

Joanna worked her way through nursing school as a single mother, after leaving an abusive first husband who was active duty Air Force. She is proud that she was able to make it on her own and be a role model for her children, and is now grateful to be in a happy second marriage, again to an Air Force member. As a nurse, Joanna has been fortunate to find work in military treatment facilities, making it easy to take her career with her to every assignment.

Emily is just resuming her career in human resources after staying home with her children for several years. She is satisfied that her patience has paid off, and that she can now finally "check the last box" by obtaining a job and having something for herself

155

again. Although she experienced frustration early in her marriage when she had to give up a job she loved for a military move, she is grateful for the life they have led and calls her husband her "Prince Charming" for rescuing her from Montana.

Olivia has been a military spouse for almost three decades, and is approaching her husband's retirement as a chief master sergeant. Although she says she's never had a continuous career, her ability to maintain employment at every assignment has been remarkable. Despite being criticized by other senior spouses along the way for working, she has continued to work, and is grateful that her husband has supported her need to be independent and fulfilled in her own right.

Vanessa

"I like being a part of something bigger than myself."

Vanessa has her own photography business and two small children. She met her husband in high school, and describes how they made the decision together for him to join the Air Force. Although it has been a roller coaster in many ways, she is proud to be a part of the military and wouldn't trade it for the world. For her, becoming a photographer was an ideal fit for her family situation and for her military life. She is able to pursue a career that is flexible enough for her to be the mother she wants to be, and she has been able to easily find clientele within her military community. Her story starts at the beginning, when she and her husband first considered a life in the military.

I had never had any sort of military experience at all. So it took a lot of prayer and thought to decide if this was the best decision for our future family. Once we looked at all the benefits and also looked at whether or not he was just going to enlist or be a commissioned officer, it was a no-brainer for us. When he joined ROTC,[16] that was great because we got benefits right away. They started paying for his school right away. They started paying for our housing, which was a big deal.

He was trying to lean toward a career where it would be a normal schedule. And they told him he'd probably deploy, but, at the time, they were 4-month deployments, maybe every couple of years. We thought, "Okay, that's doable." All the benefits, the healthcare benefits, steady employment, and the thought of traveling, for us, was actually really exciting. Coming from a really small town myself, I was ready to get out. I wanted to see the world. So we made a decision and he signed on.

---

[16]Reserve Officer Training Corps (ROTC) prepares college students to be future military officers in exchange for financial support during school.

157

From the very beginning, Vanessa and her husband demonstrate a partnership in their decision making about military life. Unlike many other spouses who began their relationships after their partners were already committed to military service, Vanessa and her husband make this commitment together. They weigh all the costs and benefits and choose military life as a team. It is not just his career having an impact on her; rather, it is a life they have chosen to create as a family unit.

I was probably more in love with the idea of just being with someone and getting ready to start a family and moving somewhere than I was about trying to pursue my own career at that point. I felt like everything would fall into place. Either I would get a job and I would do it, or I wouldn't and I would have a family. So I wasn't thinking, "Well, I need to do this. I need to have my career so how's this going to work." I wasn't career oriented at that point.

I started off working in a preschool classroom, and that was useful. I've always liked working with kids. And then, once I graduated [from college], I was able to move into [teaching] kindergarten. [At the next assignment] I still wanted to work with kids, but I wanted to focus more on children that had disorders, some sort of early intervention, or something like that. And I thought that it was going to be easy for me. I guess in my immature mindset, I was thinking that getting out of college I'm not going to have a hard time finding a job. But it took me almost 5 months to find employment and, for me, that was very frustrating.

[The job I got] was dealing with children with special needs and also children in a low-income setting and how that affects their development. [It was a] really phenomenal organization. I was able to do all kinds of things with my career. I really felt a sense of accomplishment because I found something that I had actually gone to school for and was utilizing my education. I was pursuing what I thought was my dream of working in child intervention. It was a very rewarding job. I really liked it.

[Then] we found out shortly after my son was born that my husband was going to be deploying. That was really devastating.

It was hard to tell our families, too, because they didn't want to see him leaving, plus leaving me and a new baby. That was really hard. But I had made the decision to quit working before we'd found out that he was going to deploy. I just knew that I wanted to be home and raise our children. It wasn't even an option to put them in childcare.

Here is one of the first indicators of Vanessa's ability to mindfully fit the pieces of her life together. As she describes it, she made a conscious decision to stay home with her children before becoming a parent. Her priorities were clear to her, and she recognized that her husband's deployment would add to the stress of having a new baby. For her, quitting her job at this point in time was not a difficult decision. It simply was the best fit for her life situation at that time.

From my experience, working with the 0 to 3-year-olds, I saw how devastating it was to some of these children to have their parents gone the entire week. When we had early care and late care, some of them would come in as early as they possibly could and leave as late as they possibly could. And I didn't want that for my kids. I just didn't want that, and we were financially able to make that decision for me to stay home. I was just fortunate to do that. That was solidifying for me to see these little babies being left, and I just couldn't do it.

It was good [staying home], but I started to realize that I needed to be doing something else. [However] I didn't want to be doing something that would pull me away from my kids all of the time. Actually, that's when my love of photography really started to take off. I had these cute, precious little babies, and I'm trying to capture everything I possibly can. In my ever-failing mommy brain, I'm trying to picture them in a newborn phase and I can't do it. All I can think about is the spit-up on my shirt or whatever. So I started taking snapshots, and then it developed into more stuff. I got a nicer camera and took some shots of the boys and printed them in a decent size and hung them on the wall. I got a lot of encouragement from friends and family to pursue this. Never in my mind did I think that I would go to school in developmental psychology and end up being a photographer, but it just sort of fell into place. I didn't think I'd be going back to work, but I thought I could do this.

Vanessa hadn't planned to go back to work, but was aware that she needed to do something for herself. So when she began to get into photography, the idea of starting a home-based, flexible business was appealing to her. This gave her an outlet for herself that fit her family needs as well as her military life.

I could start a business and I could travel with that business, because I could take it wherever we go. I could do it out of my home. And with the military, it wouldn't really be an issue because it was there with me. It was just a part of me. So it seemed really reasonable, something where I had a creative outlet. I could be contributing to society or be a part of something bigger than myself, still creating my own schedule. I was still able to be there for the boys when they needed me.

I thought that being the caregiver for my children would be enough for me. And it was enough, but it still felt like I needed to be doing something outside of them. I realized I still needed a piece of me that was separate from my children. I didn't want to continually see myself as a mom. You never break free from that role, but I didn't want that to be my only label. I wanted something for myself; and I needed something where I was pursuing something individually that wouldn't necessarily affect my children, but I could still go off on this career path and still feel like I was accomplishing my own goals.

As her story continues, Vanessa describes how both her marriage and military life began to take some unexpected turns. When her husband is faced with his third deployment, Vanessa's commitment to stay in the military begins to waver. This is not the deal she thought they had initially agreed to, so they decide that her husband will leave the military.

The business idea started to really grow when my husband came back from his second deployment. Then he found out a few months later that he was going to be gone for a year [on another deployment]. And I thought, "This is awful. You've already gone on two deployments, and you've only been in for a few years. This is not what we signed up for." So we made the decision that he was going to get out because it was just too much on our family. He actually submitted his paperwork and everything. Sorry, I'm going to cry.

Vanessa is crying…

But after searching and searching and trying to find something that was comparable to what he was doing, it was nearly impossible. We decided together that it wasn't going to work [financially]. We were just going to have to push through whatever deployment we were going to have to go through and he was going to stay in the military.

It was really hard seeing him as the caretaker for our family struggle so much. I didn't want that for him. I didn't want that for us. And I knew he was doing what he was supposed to be doing. As hard as that is for our family, I knew that's what he was supposed to be doing. So he pulled [back] his paperwork, and they said, "All right, but [if you stay in the Air Force] that means you're going to leave [on deployment]. You don't have a choice. You have to do this 365 [day deployment]."

Vanessa's marriage and her love for her husband are the highest priority in her decision making at this point. Although she knows a year-long deployment will be difficult, she is more concerned about her husband and his dignity and well-being. She is willing to make the sacrifice needed to allow him to succeed and continue his military service. During the year he was away, Vanessa threw herself wholeheartedly into promoting her business.

We made the decision that I would go back home and be with family. I registered [my business] with the state of Wyoming and that was a really proud moment. But I think my children probably suffered a little bit in that time because not only was their dad gone, I was sort of not there emotionally. It was hard with your husband being gone, and he was doing convoy missions in Afghanistan. That part was hard, but I think I turned that emotional part of it around and used that for fuel for my own personal thing that I was trying to do. I needed that distraction. I needed something for myself while he was gone.

Having the photography business helped Vanessa survive the year apart from her husband, and gave her an outlet she needed for herself. She also found that her business was successful, and wanted to continue on that path when they got orders to move to Germany. Here she describes what the move overseas was like for her.

I thought it was a great opportunity. I'm going to be surrounded by a military community where word of mouth within spouses is the most powerful form of advertising. I started just doing [photo shoots for] some friends and that kind of thing. But right away, it was just like wildfire. Just exactly like I thought it would be. There would be a huge need and I would have a huge target market here and it would just take off. And that's exactly what happened. At some point, especially around the holidays, I had to tell some people I couldn't take any more clients. And that was a first for me to have to tell people "no" because I was so busy. But it was really good.

I'm really, really proud of my work. I stand behind it 100%. I love being able to give people something that they love and are going to cherish forever. I think it's a priceless gift that you give to somebody. It's fantastic. I feel like I have a purpose.

Vanessa explained before the interview that the Air Force had told her to close her photography business because her home-based business on the military installation appeared to violate the requirements of the local Status of Forces Agreement (SOFA) in Germany. SOFA documents govern what is allowable for American military personnel and their dependents while living in an overseas host nation. Although the military legal office later determined that Vanessa could continue her home-based business without violating the SOFA, at the time of her interview, the future of Vanessa's business was uncertain. She did not know if she would be allowed to work again in Germany.

I feel like this has been taken away from me, like I've been cheated. There could be some kind of exception to the law. There's this stereotype that military spouses don't do anything. They kind of sit on their butts, or do whatever. They're just there as caretakers. But I feel like they [the military] almost push us to be that way instead of allowing us to do these things and be a part of these things. It's as simple as selling Pampered Chef or the other little franchise companies that military spouses are a part of. It creates camaraderie between us, and, as silly as it is, you create friendships from a Pampered Chef party. That one important person could change your life later on down the road in your military career. So, by making it so difficult, they're taking stuff away from us.

Vanessa makes a strong case for the support needed for military spouses, and the value of enabling home-based businesses to flourish. With so many obstacles to employment, especially overseas, home-based businesses are often the only viable employment option for many military spouses. Not only are these businesses sources of income, but they are also often lifelines for spouses who need a source of meaning and achievement beyond motherhood. Despite her current frustrations, Vanessa closes her story by describing how proud she is to be a part of the military community and what it means to her.

I like being a part of something bigger than myself. I like seeing my husband in this role and him being a part of something bigger than us. I think it's great and I stand by him 100%. I'm really proud of him. We went through that transition of him [possibly] getting out, and I can't see him not being in the military. I've been able to have such great friendships and meet some of the most amazing people, and become part of such an amazing family. There's a whole difference between being in a group of people that are in the military and those that are not. It's like night and day. I don't even know how to describe it, but I like being a part of that, just the sense of family that I have being a part of this. I really love it. I'm proud to be a military spouse.

For myself personally, I think the hardest part is just dealing with the rules, with the military way. This is what it is. This is what you have to do. But I wouldn't change it. I don't want to *not* be a part of this, as crazy as that is, because as sad and emotional as it has made me, a part of us will always be military. Once you get in it, you can't separate yourself from it.

Like any other military spouse, Vanessa has made personal sacrifices along the way, and she is honest about those sacrifices. Yet Vanessa has a very positive and mature way of embracing her life as a whole, the good and the bad, and accepting full responsibility to put the pieces together in the best way possible. Providing love and care for her husband and children come first for her, but she is also resolute in her decision to stand by her commitment to military service. She has embraced her love of photography and consciously created a business that not only fits her personal desires, but also integrates seamlessly with her family and military life.

Joanna

**"Life is an adventure and I think it's really cool that
I can be married to someone who is helping America stay free."**

*Joanna has been a military spouse twice, and describes her journey
from an abusive first marriage to a successful career in nursing, while
finding the "perfect" man the second time around. She is fortunate to
enjoy a good fit between her career and military life, now that she is
working in the military healthcare system. Her story begins in the days of
her first marriage when she worked part time as a seamstress to help make
ends meet.*

I had my own business as a seamstress. I did uniforms and
I had a lot of people that I'd met and had contact with. I got to do it
out of my house and always had money, which was nice –
especially when you're eking [it out] between paychecks.

I saw myself number one as the mom and spouse, and number
two as the worker. I was able to contribute to the family income, as
well as make sure that my house was nice and my kids were taken
care of, and I was not missing anything there.

I was in a very abusive relationship [though]. I picked a day,
and I sat him down and I said, "I'm going to leave you and this is
the reason why. I can't deal with this anymore." My kids saw him
hit me. My kids definitely saw him treating me terribly and that's
not who I am. I let myself get that way. That's not right. And it's a
shame that more people don't stand up for themselves. At that
point, I thought, "You know what? Screw you. I'm standing up for
myself. I'm done with you." I put the money away, set up a place
to stay, set up a job, and got the hell out of Dodge.

I was poor. I tell you, I was dirt poor going through nursing
school with three children under the age of 5. My mom even said,
"Why am I going to help you? You're going to fail anyway." I think
she did that to piss me off to the point where I would say, "I'm
going to prove you wrong, lady!" I proved everybody wrong. I got

out of a nursing school with a B average. I aced not just my exit exam, but my boards [as well].

I felt a strong sense of accomplishment and I felt very proud of myself, because that's a hard thing. If you ever went through nursing school, that's a bear. I was able to prove [something] to my kids. I know that they're young, but I was able to show my kids, "You know what? I don't have to sit back and collect welfare and collect food stamps, and just be. I did something with myself. I got up and I fought."

Joanna's sense of pride and realization of her self-worth is inspiring. Her professional accomplishments not only allowed her to take care of herself and her family, but proved to her that she was worthy and valuable, a feeling she did not derive from her first marriage. Becoming a nurse offered a source of meaning and self-esteem for Joanna that she continues to build upon. She goes on to describe what this meant to her when she got her first nursing job.

I was in the nursing part of a rehab [center] where you're really doing intense nursing. It was fabulous. I really loved it. It was awesome...I mean, it was fabulous because you had that sense of worth. You were worth something. You did something. You accomplished something.

Coming from a place where I was told for 7 years that I wasn't worth spit, it's kind of nice to actually have that worth and know in my heart that I was worth something. I mean, I accomplished [raising] three children. I accomplished [maintaining] a house. I accomplished all the things that go along with being a military spouse, and helping others, and making friends, and making money, and being the best spouse I was able to be for that person. But it's quite an accomplishment when you see it literally on paper. You have a license in your hands. You get to have letters after your name. Nobody can take that away from you.

At this point in her life, Joanna is in a good place. She has reached her professional goals, has a meaningful job, and is providing for her family as a single mother. After struggling for many years emotionally and financially, she has finally found satisfaction and stability, a life that fits for her. Then she meets her current husband, and finds herself becoming a military spouse once again.

I met the best guy in the world. He's awesome. The decision to marry him was very easy, to be honest with you. It was probably one of the easiest decisions I've ever had in my life, because he was perfect. And he accepted me. He accepted the package that came along, which were my kids. So, the decision [to move to Ohio with him] was very easy. I'm not opposed to moving. I feel it's an adventure.

It was very important for me to work and to bring in money so I can be a contributor to the household...My husband did make enough, but I felt like a leech if I wasn't working. I know it sounds really bad, but there's no reason at all that I would be staying home. What would be the logic behind that when I'm an able-bodied person that is able to go out and [practice] my craft?

I have this fear of being poor because I was so poor for so long. And, looking back, seeing that person that had to sell her jewelry, I never want to get in that position again. So if I'm able bodied, I'm going to go out and work. I like to work. It's fun. I really enjoy it. That's my reasoning. I took a huge pay cut [in Ohio], but I felt it was worth it because I got to be with an amazing person who's not just a great husband, but a great father [as well].

I maneuvered enough that I worked two 16-hour [shifts] and one 8-hour shift in 3 days. I was able to do all of that and then be home the whole [rest of the] week with my kids and my family, and take care of what needed to be done. Unfortunately, we didn't do much on the weekends because Friday, Saturday, and Sunday were the days that I worked. But it kept the other days free.

Joanna acknowledges that she did not have to continue working after she married her husband, but offers several important reasons why working was important to her. Not only did she enjoy being a nurse, but it also provided an extra sense of security to protect her from being financially vulnerable or dependent again. For her, continuing to work as a military spouse was a good fit for her life. She goes on to describe their next PCS to South Dakota.

167

Looking for a job was actually very easy. I fell into the job that I had wanted. I started working [at the base hospital] very soon after I got to South Dakota, which was nice. It's amazing when you're that close [to work] how much time you have. I'd get to work at 7:15 a.m., leave work at 4:30 p.m., and be home by 4:33. My kids were home. It was great. I was able to have my little flow and everything worked well. I worked there until my husband deployed for a year, which was very hard. But we got through it. I was just exhausted. I was tired because I didn't just work. I also did Officers' Spouses Club [OSC]. I was on the board for that. I ran a support group. I went to school. I volunteered at the thrift store. What else did I do? I took care of the kids. I took care of the dogs – we had two dogs at that time. I was still volunteering as a quasi-key spouse[17] [as well].

But I loved what I did. I really did. I loved helping the community. I loved the part that I got to help the military community – and not just the active duty, the dependents, and their children. I got to help the retired people. It was kind of neat seeing the retired people coming through. I said, "Wow, what they've seen." It was very gratifying.

During this second assignment, Joanna fully embraces her role as a military spouse. Not only does she continue to work full time, but also finds herself a temporary single mom again while her husband deploys. Neither of those roles stop her, however, from taking up several volunteer roles in the military community. She admits she was exhausted at times from trying to do so much, but she clearly finds her life to be rewarding and happy. Her journey continues with a third PCS, to Germany this time, where she lands a nursing position in an obstetrics (OB) clinic at the base hospital.

I learned German in high school. I took 4 years in it, and I always wanted to go and live overseas. I thought that would be quite an adventure. I always think of our moves as little adventures.

---

[17] The Air Force "Key Spouse" role is meant to serve as a resource and informal source of support for other military spouses within an Air Force unit.

Literally, we got here [to Germany], and within a few days, I went to [the hospital] with resume in hand and said, "I'm getting a job." [I handed in] my paperwork and they said, "Where do you want to work?"

When I [first started working in the OB clinic], I worked with someone I called "Salty." That's the only way to describe her. She was downright mean. I won't lie to you. I cried every day when I left work. I said, "I just want to quit." But I had finally gotten into the government system and [my husband] said, "If you quit now, that kills you for the rest of your life for a government job. Just stick it out." I was just miserable. Eventually, Salty got orders and she's gone now. Thank God, she's gone.

I see myself a little bit stronger, obviously, because I survived that really hard first year. That was the hardest. And my husband didn't cave to me saying, "I am so done." It's funny because I go to work every day now. I get there before 7:00 a.m., even though my shift doesn't start until 7:30. I don't usually leave until about 5:00 p.m. and my shift ends at 4:30. Sometimes I don't take lunch because you have somebody who needs help. You're there and it's really nice…I'm very proud of what I do.

Joanna is tested by her initial work experience in Germany. Although she is tempted to leave a toxic work environment, she does not want to be short sighted and sacrifice the long-term stability of her career and military life. For her, the situation resolves itself and she is once again happy and fulfilled at work. Furthermore, she recognizes that being a part of the GS system is a huge benefit to her that allows her to integrate her career with military life with each move.

It's hard when you have to start from scratch. That's why I'm happy I'm in the military system now. I can transfer and I'm not going to be at the bottom of the totem pole anymore. The only thing that is bad about working, I will say, is the fact that a lot of places have this misconception that officers' spouses shouldn't work. It's an old way of thinking, a very depressing way of thinking because what are they going to do?

I'm getting this perception because a lot of things that I wanted to do are catered to women who don't work. I wanted to join the Officers' Spouses Club here, [and they said] "We have nighttime meetings." But there's only been one. I can't take time off to be at your meetings in the morning and, I'm sorry, but people do have jobs. I [am also a] key spouse. [People ask] "Well, why don't we [meet] at lunchtime?" I work and sometimes I don't get lunches. So, it's all of that in my face saying, "Why do you work?"

It really upsets me and I have now boycotted the OSC, which I know I shouldn't do, but I'm very annoyed with them telling me one thing and doing another. It's very frustrating for me. There are people who like to participate who can't because they work and I'm one of them. I love doing that kind of thing, and I love knowing people who are outside of my work. I love the people I work with but I don't have any real friends here. And I kind of miss that. I don't have that anymore because by the time I get home from work, and do everything I need to do, and run around the kids, I'm tired.

But the thing is, if you want to have something that's supporting the military and supporting the spouses, [then] why don't you make it so everybody can attend and not just a select few? That's the thing that upsets me.

Although Joanna has successfully integrated her career, family, and military life, she acknowledges here that there are still sacrifices. There is still a traditional military spouse culture (especially in overseas locations where many spouses are unable to work) that focuses on daytime social activities and volunteerism. As a result, Joanna feels excluded from her community, which she loves and was eager to participate in. Joanna closes her interview with some thoughts about why she loves the military way of life so much.

My dad being in the military, growing up that way, and having him going away is all I know and I don't know any different. Growing up, my father was a huge influence on me. My dad was a Vietnam vet and retired from the Air Force reserves a few years ago. It's odd to me if you don't put a uniform on every day. I guess

I'm not normal. I like that I can support my husband and I can support the lifestyle that we have. We have this certain lifestyle and we move and we pick up and make a life in 15 different places. I'd get bored if I had to stay in one spot.

Life is an adventure and I think it's really cool that I can be married to someone who is helping America stay free. Having that patriotic way of thought for something bigger than you is kind of neat. It's really a neat thing that my husband gets to defend my freedom, as well as a lot of people's freedoms, and [that I can] be part of something bigger than I am. And, the funny thing is, he can go and get a job wherever in the states, and get paid double the amount, but he chooses to be in the military because he likes it.

Like Vanessa in the previous story, Joanna feels a strong commitment to military service. Perhaps it is easier for her to find a fit among the various roles in her life because, at the core, she believes so strongly in what her husband does. There is no conflict between her values and purpose and those of her husband. In that way, her marriage is perfectly aligned with a military life. Fortunately, Joanna also happens to be in a portable career field that is further simplified by her entry into the GS system, enabling her to make PCS moves less disruptive for her career. Finally, although Joanna does not talk in much detail about her current parenting demands, she does not cite any stressors caused by military life. If anything, becoming a military spouse has lightened the load she used to feel as a single parent. In some ways, Joanna has been lucky that circumstances have come together to form a good life for her, but she has also worked very hard to create those circumstances and mindfully craft the best life possible for herself and her family.

Emily

**"Finally, this is like the perfect ending to the story.
Just check the box. You are in."**

*Originally from Russia, Emily moved to Montana when she was 18
years old and says that experience prepared her for the adventure of
military life. Although moving around has delayed her career progression
in the human resources field, she has just landed her first GS job that she
hopes will put her on a long-term, portable career path. She says it feels
like "checking the last box," and she is happy that her life now feels
complete. She starts by describing her time in Montana, when she first
met her husband.*

When I was working in Montana, I was working as a social
worker and I became a good friend with one girl. Her husband and
my [now] husband were best friends. They introduced us [to each
other]. [After we got married] I just quit my job to move with my
husband [who was in Spokane, Washington]. I wasn't really
planning to work until we moved to a different duty station
because he only had one year left. But then I just became bored, so
I applied to the CDC and got a job because it seemed to me this was
the easiest job I could have gotten. I applied to the CDC and worked
there for about a year until we PCSed [to Washington, DC].

I started working in downtown DC. That was my first human
resources job. I wanted to do something different and human
resources was something I was interested in. I loved my job so
much – meeting new people, having this busy schedule, [doing]
payroll, and [enjoying] the people I worked with. It was just a good
environment. It was just perfect. If you describe your perfect job
where you feel like you want to get up [every morning] and go, that
would be it. That's why I liked that place. The boss, the president
of the company, was great. He was taking care of his employees,
and my pay was good.

[I felt] good, like I was going up the ladder, a ladder I wanted to start climbing. I felt like I accomplished things. I was really happy with my job position, the people I was working with, the responsibilities I had to do. Honestly, my husband knows that if he was not in the military, I really would like to be a professional. I would really love to make a career in human resources. I was real upset to leave [that job] because now I feel like every time [we move], I have to start from the bottom. I didn't want to go [to Misawa, Japan].

I always wanted a career, but being married to a military man, you know you have to sacrifice something. I'm happy where I am, but for your own satisfaction that you did something in life you want to say, "I have a degree and I'm a professional." That's important to me. I don't know why. I think everybody wants to be successful in life.

At this stage of her story, Emily believes it is inevitable that she will have to sacrifice her career, at least somewhat, because of her husband's military service. She is understanding, but also frustrated, after having a job in Washington, DC, that piqued her interest in the human resources field. Although she is disappointed, she is also pragmatic in her point of view. During her next two assignments, Japan and Turkey, Emily has two children and becomes a stay-at-home mom. She retains her career dreams at some level, but is also flexible enough to shift her short-term focus to other priorities.

It was just a different job, staying at home, and I figured I'm still going to try to apply for a GS position. So I was fine. Plus, I didn't trust anybody to take care of my kids when they were that age. Even if I had a job, I don't think I would be going back to work so soon.

For some reason, we have been so lucky with our assignments. Every assignment we've been happy about, and every time we were ready to go. We were ready to start from the beginning because we enjoy the change of scenery. Even with my job in DC, we were ready to go. We wanted adventure, especially when we found out we were going to Japan. We can just travel and enjoy.

I still think I loved my job in DC. It's been 6 years? I still think that was the best employment I had. But I can't think, "Oh, I wish I stayed there." That's not what I chose. I chose to be married to a military guy, so something better will come up.

I was thinking that if I get a GS position, I will be able to go up [the ladder]. So when we go to Germany, hopefully there are going to be more jobs and I'm just going to start applying for a GS position.

Over the years, Emily is able to maintain a long-term view of her life goals. She enjoys the adventure of each new assignment, and recognizes the value of staying home while her children are young, but still keeps a future goal of employment in the GS system. She is patient and waits for the right time to return to work, while still enjoying the journey along the way. Now in Germany, Emily explains that she has just accepted a job offer for a human resources position in the GS system.

I'm excited, but I was also doing good [before the job offer]. I was enjoying it because I like to exercise. When I drop off my kids, I go exercise. I do some grocery [shopping]. I do whatever, clean the house – you know, just "me" time. But I can't say no to a job in HR. [I can] get that experience, so I can start climbing the ladder in [the] GS [system]. At least, in the back of my mind, I know that I will have [military spouse] preference when I go to a new place to get a job. It will be much easier for me to get a job, if I want it. So it just gives [me] that feeling of security, "Okay, that's it. I'm in."

I [hope to get] that fulfillment that I'm back being a career woman. It's not like I have anything against stay-at-home moms, but I always knew that I'm not going to stay home forever. I always knew that I'm going to start looking for a job and I just want to be busy. I just want to do something besides clean the house and take care of my kids. I love my kids. But it's my time that I go and I do something. And I still want to go up the ladder.

It makes me happy. I don't know how to explain it. Inside of me, it's like a "check box." And now that checks the box in me. The kids are taken care of, and every aspect of my life seems good. We are in Germany, and we are enjoying it. There are all these little check boxes, and then there's this thing like, "What am I going to do with myself?" Finally, this is like the perfect ending to the story. Just check the box. You are in.

Emily is very rational in her perspective. She set out to claim a job in HR and got one. This was the last big remaining thing on her life list of important things to do, and she is satisfied that she can now check that box. She explains how getting this job will put her on the career path she has been dreaming about for a long time. At the same time, on an emotional level, she recognizes there will be some loss of freedom when she returns to work. She will lose the flexibility she has to exercise, take care of household chores, and get time to herself. In her rational calculations, it is worth it for her to give up this freedom, despite the feelings of loss she is sure to experience. Overall, Emily has a positive outlook about her future and is pleased with her life as a whole.

I hear these people talking about their bad days, but to me we are lucky. We're lucky on all our assignments. We were lucky that we got our degrees before [having] kids. We did that check box. I'm happy with our military career and myself. There's nowhere to go for me. It's taken care of.

My husband was my Prince Charming who came and rescued me [from Montana]. He took me out of that hole. No offense to anybody from Montana. He took me out of that hole and just pretty much said, "Here, do whatever you want." And he has always been supportive of me. That's important too. He's always been supportive with me getting an education. He was supporting me not having a job if that's what I wanted. And he's happy that I'm happy.

Emily's closing line is a perfect testimony to the way her marriage fits into her story. "He's happy that I'm happy." While she has been sorting out her career goals and plans, she has been comforted by the fact that her husband will always support any choice that makes her happy. That knowledge gives her the added freedom to examine all of her choices and pick the best alternative for her at each point in time. In Washington, DC, it was right for her to work. While they lived overseas and their children were young, it was right for her to stay home. Now that she feels ready to

Michelle Still Mehta

return to work, her husband supports that too. Although Emily may have preferred a more continuous career path, she has always maintained a positive outlook and recognizes that she is lucky to have a supportive spouse and a military lifestyle that she and her family enjoy. With eyes wide open, she has patiently waited for the right time to return to work and choose a position that will help her advance in the GS system, giving her the portability she needs and desires.

Olivia

"I always had my own sense of self-worth and my own sense of independence."

Olivia's husband is approaching retirement after a 30-year career in the Air Force. With 11 assignments under her belt, and a new job with almost every one, Olivia wishes she had been able to have what she considers to be a continuous career rather than a series of jobs. However, she is proud of her accomplishments and feels good that her husband has always supported her efforts. Olivia begins her interview by reflecting on her overall experience and how her working life has unfolded.

I don't think that I've ever had a career. I have a job, and there's a big difference. I have nothing invested anywhere, except in my family and my marriage. When my husband gets out of the military, he'll have done 30 years. He'll have invested his entire life, his retirement, his everything. He has a connection there. I don't have that. I have a connection to the military by being [around the] military every single day of my life. My father was a Marine, then I was in the Air Force, and then I married [my husband]. But I've never had a career.

It wasn't until later on in our life together that it hit me when I would leave jobs that I really liked, because I've had a few. I can honestly say I've been very lucky. Ninety-nine percent of the jobs that I've had I really regretted leaving. There are a couple [jobs where] I was ready to go after a while, but I stayed for the money. I've been lucky. I've been able to work everywhere I go because I'm so diverse in my skills. I've had to be. I've learned to be. I don't have the education, though, because I left college to go into the Air Force, and I've never gone back.

I've always worked, even in high school and college. I've always had that sense of freedom, having my own money, not feeling so dependent. I think that was a big thing. I didn't have that sense of guilt for being at home sitting there, feeling like I wasn't doing anything, while he's out working so hard making all the money for the house. I was able to contribute, knowing that if we go out and we spend money, it's not putting a strain on our finances because I was contributing too. And that's important to me.

Olivia's first overseas assignment with her husband turned out to be a pivotal experience. With two toddlers of her own, and few employment opportunities, she decided to work as a babysitter while she was home with her own children. This turned out to be a bad fit for Olivia.

When we went to Izmir, Turkey, I had an 18-month-old and a 3½-year-old at that point. I met a lady there and she was a GS employee. Her husband was [in the] Army and they had a 3½-year-old who needed a babysitter. So I said, "Oh, well, until I get a job, I'll watch him." He was a terror, a holy terror. He broke our sliding glass window with his head, and it didn't faze him at all. That's when I told my husband, "I can't do this. I am so miserable here. I'm literally stuck in the house with three kids all day long every day. I can't do this." He said, "First off, you need to quit babysitting him." So I did. They found childcare for him. And then he said, "You need to get a job. You're happier when you work."

I didn't want the girls in daycare because it was way too expensive for two in daycare. I got a job working at the NCO [Non-Commissioned Officer] Club as one of the head cashiers from 5:00 to 9:00 in the evening. [My husband would] get off at 4:00 p.m. and come home. We'd switch places and he'd take care of the girls in the evening. He would feed them, bathe them, and get them in bed while I went to work for 4 hours. It seemed to make a world of difference.

I had that sense of independence. I didn't feel trapped. I didn't feel completely dependent upon him. I had adult interaction. I had adult conversation. I was my own person again. I took care of the kids during the day and took care of the house, and then I was my own person for those 4 hours a day. It made the year and a half we had left there fly by; and it turned out to be a great assignment, but I was miserable for [those] first 6 months.

Olivia's husband recognized that she was unhappy and identified what was missing in her life by saying, "You're happier when you work." Not only was he conscious of her needs, but he followed up those words with real action. He made the commitment to be home every day on time so that he could be the caretaker while Olivia went to work. This event symbolizes the core of Olivia's marriage – her freedom to be an independent and whole person. She explains the difference between being an independent military spouse and a "dependent wife."

There is a difference between being a military spouse and a dependent wife. You picture these women who go to the commissary[18] and they'll throw a fit about something stupid. Or they go to the clinic and demand to be seen because of who their husband is or what their status is in the community. It always seems their entire life was negative, and it all revolved around their husband, their status, their position, and their job. It was never about them. They didn't seem to have their own identity and I never wanted to be a "dependent wife." I wanted my own identity. I wanted my own sense of self-worth. And, [during] the first 6 months in Turkey, even though I was helping another military family take care of their child, I didn't have a sense of self-worth.

Not that I'm thinking a stay-at-home mom is bad, because there are absolutely wonderful stay-at-home moms. Their whole purpose in life, or their whole world, revolves around their home, their spouse, their children – and that's perfectly fine for them. That's just not fine for me. And I realize that. I recognize that and I'm happier when I'm working.

Olivia feels strongly that having a job while being a mother and military spouse is the best fit for her. Working not only makes her happier, but also gives her a greater sense of purpose and self-worth. The types of jobs Olivia held varied at different assignments. In England, she worked as a school secretary.

---

[18] The Defense Commissary Agency (DeCA) operates commissaries on military installations where military members and their families can purchase groceries and household goods.

In England, it was more [about having] something to do, something to keep me occupied so I'm not sitting at home, not doing anything. I can't do that. That bothers me. I think if I didn't have those jobs, I would have felt more useless, being at home, especially when the kids were older. You get up, you clean the house, you make the bed, you do the laundry, and then what? What's left? I don't have a whole lot of hobbies, so to spend all day knitting or to spend all day reading a love story…I would literally be sitting there, bored stiff. And I've done that a couple of times. Then I went out and got a job.

I don't think I know anybody who wants to sit there and feel useless. I'm certain that everybody wants to feel like they have a purpose, like there's a reason for them to get up every morning. I just needed something more outside of the house for me, to keep me occupied, to give me a sense of self-worth, and not financial worth. Everybody wants to feel needed. Once the house is clean and the kids are in school, they don't need you anymore.

Again, Olivia emphasizes the importance of purpose. Having a job makes her feel needed in a way that unpaid work at home does not. After several more moves and jobs, Olivia found herself in New Jersey as an empty nester, and got a job working for the company that managed the housing on base.

By that time, both of my children were gone. And it was hard for me at first. I didn't want to be at home when we went to New Jersey because the day after my youngest went to college, we packed up and moved there. I got a job so I wasn't sitting at home all the time, so I had something to occupy my time. And it wasn't for the money. It was for something to do. Within 3 months, I was promoted to one of the managers and got a huge raise. That was the hardest thing I ever walked away from when we moved [to Germany] because I never thought, as an uneducated woman, I would ever make $50,000 a year. It was so good!

Oliva surprised herself by earning more than she ever thought she would. Although working had always been important to her as a source of purpose and independence, she had never felt like she was really pursuing a career. Suddenly, this big raise shocks her and demonstrates how far she has come over the course of her working life. Feeling a bit ashamed that she never finished her college degree, she is now redeemed a bit by reaching this milestone. Now in Germany, Olivia has an administrative job at the hospital and explains what work means to her now that her husband is approaching retirement.

Before [when the kids were growing up], I had something at home to keep me occupied, but it wasn't fulfilling enough. Now, I don't want to go back home and sit there and do nothing. I want to be busy; but it's more important for me to make the money, knowing that in a year, we're going to be retiring. Right now, we live off of my income and we bank his. We put money away for a cruise this summer with our girls. One last trip before my daughter gets married and we're paying for the wedding. We have been able to pay for their colleges, both of them, and we've paid their cars off, so they're walking out of college with no debt. That's important to us. So now I'm back to working for the money. I'm not back to working for the satisfaction of working.

Although Olivia contends she does not have a "career," she is now the primary breadwinner for their family. Humbly, she says they are living off her income and banking her husband's. She doesn't particularly like her current job, but is proud that she is able to contribute to her family and help with some very important milestones, like her daughters' weddings and educations. Olivia goes on to talk about some of the real sacrifices she has had to make as a military spouse and the lessons she tried to teach her daughters along the way.

My husband and his career truly are the most important things to me, because they've had to be. He has risen to the highest rank he can rise to as an enlisted member. He has a master's degree, and [when he was] getting that, I helped pick up the slack at home. I took care of the kids a little bit more. I did all the running around. We sacrificed as a family to get him where he is, but it's been tough, too, because I've had some really good jobs that I really loved. I feel that his career has been more important, above and beyond anything else. If he wanted to try a new job, we would go. There have been times when I'm really happy in my job and I'm having to leave a home that I love, a job that I love, my friends, my church, my family, so he can fulfill his adventure. That's been tough. I think that's been the hardest. And maybe that's a reason why I do work, because I want there to be something else that is just me outside of the home. Because he has his something else. He has his career.

I always had my own sense of self-worth and my own sense of independence. And I had my own little work world. I had my own life. And that was important to me. I was me. I was my own person. I wanted [my girls] to see the importance [of my working] because it taught them a sense of self-independence and a sense of self-worth. I always taught them, "You are your own person." What you do with your life is your choice. And you can either choose to be with someone or you can choose to be by yourself, but you need to make sure you can take care of *you*. Don't rely on anyone else to take care of you because, when you start relying on somebody else to take care of you financially, then you get stuck with somebody that you're not meant to be with. And you have no way out. Always have a way out.

Olivia places a high value on her sense of independence and wants her daughters to have the same freedom she has had. Although she has willingly made personal sacrifices to make her husband's career primary, she has never lost sight of the need for her to be able to take care of herself. Her advice to always have a way out is not a critique of her own marriage, but rather insight into an essential ingredient to living a healthy and whole individual life. As she wraps up her interview, Olivia laments that some military spouses do not share her views, and that a culture still exists that discourages spouses from working.

I think it's hard for me justifying why I work because there are so many women that don't. And I don't look down on them for not working, but the higher my husband went in his rank and the more prestigious his position became, some women couldn't understand why I worked. [For example] when he became the command chief, they introduced me to the president of the Enlisted Spouses' Club. I had never been involved in the spouses' club before and I was going to be their advisor. What was I going to advise them on? I didn't even know where the spouses' club was because the military was not my focus. It just wasn't. It was where he worked. I had a whole other life outside of the military, and I was happy about that. [The club president] came up to me and said, "Oh, I've heard about you. I hear you work full time." I'm thinking, "Out of everything they could have told her about me, that was the one thing she focused on?"

Just because I work outside the home doesn't mean I'm not involved in my husband's career. When we moved to New Jersey, one of the ladies asked him, "Well, is [your wife] going to work when she gets to New Jersey?" And he said I probably would, because I'd always worked. And she said, "Well, that's too bad. Maybe it would help your career a little bit more if she didn't work." How much more could I help his career by staying at home, waiting for him to come home?

Like Joanna, Olivia has found working to be a good fit with her military life, but has sometimes encountered obstacles from other spouses. Although she has crafted a life that works for her, Olivia has bucked the traditional norm of being the supportive spouse who stays home. That norm is gradually changing, but Olivia's experience demonstrates that some outdated notions are still alive and well. Luckily, throughout their military journey, Olivia and her husband have consistently been on the same page.

Thank God I have a husband who doesn't want me to be submissive. He wants me to be my own person, have my own individuality, because I'm not happy when I don't feel that. I feel like there's something missing in my life, because it's my own little piece of life. And if that's missing, I don't feel whole. I don't feel complete. I feel like I'm not doing what I'm meant to do on this earth. I needed that, and he recognizes that, and he's tried really hard to make these moves as easy as possible on me.

Sometimes it's hard. I always give him the analogy, "When you have an assignment change, you pick up your coffee cup on your desk and you set it on the next desk, and you're there. I have a house I have to pack up and unpack. I have children I have to pull out of school and deal with them leaving their friends and the church and leaving everything behind and getting them settled in a new home. I have to deal with all of that while you go off to your office. I'm there dealing with all of that."

Olivia is a success story, yet she admits the sacrifices have been real. She has carried most of the burden whenever her husband gets a new assignment. She shepherds the family through the change and reinvents her own career, while her husband moves his coffee cup to his new desk. Although that image is certainly an oversimplification, it is symbolic of the role Olivia and many military spouses play during a PCS. While military members maintain their identity, rank, and career field most of the time, spouse careers and support systems are often entirely uprooted and rebuilt each time. Olivia has mastered the art of resilience by landing a job with every assignment and being flexible enough to forge a creative career path, all while being a strong role model for her daughters. She has learned to fit employment with military life, even if she is unwilling to call her job history a career necessarily. At the heart of it all is a strong woman who believes in herself, and a life partner who deeply cares about her happiness.

Lessons on Integrating the 3 Ms

The four stories in this chapter exemplify integration of the 3 Ms because each of these women has mindfully worked to craft a life that fits for her. They have all faced the typical challenges any military spouse faces, but have been fortunate to find individual paths that work for them. The following are some of the lessons I take away from their stories:

1. **Integrating the 3 Ms requires true partnership.** Nobody in this chapter made life or career decisions on their own. Each of the four stories includes a marriage where two people make supportive decisions in partnership with each other. Perhaps, more importantly, each woman in this chapter expresses gratitude for her partner in some way. For example, Olivia is thankful that her husband always encouraged her to work and wanted her to be her own person, even when other spouses were critical of her choices. Emily feels like her husband saved her by taking her away from Montana and says that her husband simply supports her desire to be happy. Joanna says that marrying her husband was the easiest decision of her life; he was a perfect fit for her. Vanessa and her husband have made joint decisions every step of the way, including the decision to enter the Air Force in the first place. It is clear from these stories that a strong marriage is the basic foundation of the 3 Ms.

2. **Integrating the 3 Ms includes honoring your own needs as a mother.** Not only do these women testify to strong marriages, but they are equally strong in their convictions about motherhood. They all know what matters to them as a parent, and have made choices that enable them to play that role effectively. After working with infants at a childcare center, Vanessa had a strong desire to stay home

185

while her children were young. Her plans to become a photographer only worked because they fit her life as a mother. Joanna is proud that she taught her children the value of being self-sufficient and never wavered in her commitment to model that as a working mother. Emily is pragmatic in her approach to parenting, saying that she looked at motherhood as her job while her children were young. Because that was her primary job for a period of time, she felt no conflict in staying out of the workforce. Olivia, on the other hand, recognized that she did not do well as a stay-at-home mom. She needed to work outside of the house to preserve an outlet for herself and be happy.

3. **Integrating the 3 Ms is easier when you are committed to military life, despite all its unique challenges.** Each of the women in this chapter also expressed strong support for military life, perhaps making it easier for them to endure the hardships that cropped up from time to time. Olivia grew up in a military family and joined the Air Force herself before becoming a military spouse. Vanessa initially chose military life when her husband joined ROTC, and later chose it again when they considered getting out, recognizing this was the best path for her husband's well-being. Joanna also comes from a military family and speaks patriotically about the value of serving our country. While Emily did not grow up in the United States, she is grateful for the opportunities the military has offered her. Each of these women sees military life as noble and worthy, and is committed to the joint decision she and her husband have made to serve.

4. **Integrating the 3 Ms includes finding a sustainable career path.** The women in this chapter all have very different career paths, demonstrating that there is no single best answer to spouse employment. The most important thing

they hold in common is that they found a path that works for them. They found a fit between career and the 3 Ms. Olivia chose to seek a new job at each and every assignment, claiming it wasn't really a career, but it did allow her to progress and earn an increasing salary over time. Vanessa chose self-employment to enjoy the flexibility she needed at home, and the portability she needed for future military moves. She also picked a line of business that fit perfectly within a military community so she could market herself to fellow military spouses. As a nurse, Joanna locked in the portability of her career once she became a GS employee and has been able to work at military treatment facilities when they PCS to a new location. Emily has patiently waited for her time to return to the workforce in human resources, hoping that her new GS position will give her the portable career she has been hoping for.

5. **Integrating the 3 Ms takes resilience and grace, without compromising who you are.** None of the women in this chapter have a perfect story to tell. They have all hit roadblocks, some of them very challenging, yet they have demonstrated the grace and resilience needed to accept those challenges and overcome them. Vanessa was challenged by repeated deployments but found that her photography business actually saved her sanity in some ways. Joanna was forced to overcome an abusive first husband and work her way out of poverty before finding stability and happiness in her current marriage. Emily was disappointed to leave her ideal job in human resources, but waited patiently for the right time and place in her life to get back on track. Olivia tenaciously reinvented herself at each assignment, and held various jobs ranging from club cashier, to school nurse, to property manager, to healthcare administrator. All of these women learned creative ways of accommodating military life, but none of them were ever

willing to compromise their sense of self. Each woman has a strong sense of who she is and what she values, and the changing circumstances of her military life did not change that. If anything, they all became more resolved to be true to themselves and to remain unwavering in the paths they chose.

6. **Integrating the 3 Ms is not a one-time event, but a constant process of renegotiation.** Unfortunately, this process of making our lives fit into a healthy whole is not a one-time problem to solve. As our lives and relationships change, so too must we adjust and realign the various pieces and parts to preserve the fit we seek. Vanessa thought her military life was a good fit when she agreed to sign up, but found it difficult to sustain when her husband deployed several times. She had to realign her approach to military life in order to stay on track. Joanna came close to leaving her GS position in Germany because of a toxic supervisor, but suffered through one difficult year in order to keep the tenure she did not want to lose. For the sake of staying in the GS system, she pushed through this challenging time. Emily gave up the first position she held in human resources because of a PCS move, believing that it was more important to be with her husband than to keep that particular job. But she held onto that position as an ideal she would come back to someday. Olivia initially thought that staying home was the right answer for her when she had young children, until her husband suggested she needed a job to get her out of the house. Understanding that need changed her definition of what fit for her and her life.

Questions for Reflection

The stories in this chapter offer the best examples of individual spouses who have successfully integrated the 3 Ms. Although there are many elements of success in the stories included in previous chapters, these four stood out for me as women who mindfully navigated the complexities of their lives and did so with a sense of grace and acceptance. I hope you will take this time to reflect on your own capability to do the same. Take a look at the following questions and pick one or two that resonate with you. Explore your answers to those questions through personal journaling or by talking with a friend or your spouse.

1. How well have you integrated your 3 Ms? Where do you need to make changes?
2. Do you have a true partnership at the foundation of your 3 Ms? If not, what is missing? What are you grateful for in your partner?
3. How well have you lived up to your own expectations of motherhood or fatherhood? What would you change?
4. How committed are you to military life? Do you and your spouse agree on how long he/she will stay in?
5. How resilient are you in responding to challenges that come up? Where would you like to find more grace and acceptance?
6. How easily are you able to renegotiate your 3 Ms when changes occur (e.g., PCS moves, deployments, family needs, job changes)?
7. In what ways do you want to grow or change during your military journey? What parts of yourself do you want to preserve and build upon?

Chapter 6 – A Call to Action

All 21 stories in this book are a combination of triumph and struggle, hope and despair. Some of these women have been tested more than others. Some have shown amazing resiliency, optimism, and grace in the face of their struggles, while others are still trying to find a positive path forward. None of these are perfect success stories, and each woman has the potential to find greater fit and harmony in their lives.

The 3 M framework is just one lens to use when looking at these stories, but is a useful tool for any military spouse trying to sort out his or her career within the context of a military life. Ultimately, this approach is a coping strategy to help individual spouses thrive in their military lives. The 3 Ms will not remedy the root causes of the spouse employment problem, even if it is an effective way for an individual spouse to find peace in the short run. Unless we begin to seriously address the sources of this widespread problem, we will be stuck repeating this cycle far into the future. Not only is that wrong, but it is unsustainable for an all-volunteer force that is already struggling to retain the talent needed for the future of our military.

I am struck by how much attention has been given to spouse employment in the past decade. When I was a new spouse 18 years ago, I found few resources or role models for career-oriented spouses. Now there are a growing number of initiatives in public and private sectors promoting military spouse employment. From the Military Spouse Employment Partnership (MSEP)[19] within DoD, to the creation of Blue Star Families, and the introduction of

---

[19] MSEP partners with private employers who have pledged to support the hiring of military spouses, and their website includes a job search portal that lists opportunities with these employers:
https://msepjobs.militaryonesource.mil/msep/home.

legislation[20] to promote military spouse employment opportunities, there is a steady growth of programs in this arena. These initiatives have created a surge in awareness about the employment challenges faced by spouses and have prompted employers to commit to hiring from the military spouse community. In addition, the range of resources now available to job-searching spouses is greater than ever and growing by the day.[21]

Root Causes of the Problem

Despite the recent well-intentioned wave of support, military spouse unemployment and underemployment have shown little improvement. As discussed in Chapter 1, the primary obstacles to employment consistently cited by military spouses are service member job demands (including relocations and deployments), family obligations, and childcare (Blue Star Families, 2016a). My belief is that these issues will not show any real improvement until action is taken to address three root causes of the spouse employment problem:

1. An outdated military culture
2. Gender inequality
3. A broken and inefficient personnel assignment system

---

[20] Senator Tim Kaine of Virginia sponsored the Military Spouse Employment Act of 2018, which is intended to promote federal hiring of spouses, ease restrictions on home-based businesses on military installations, and provide additional resources for education, training, and childcare.

[21] Career resources are constantly evolving and too numerous to list here, but are offered by a variety of sources, including DoD-wide programs, installation-level programs through family support/readiness organizations, and a vast number of nonprofit organizations dedicated to serving military families. If you are looking for information about resources, DoD's Military OneSource is a good place to start: https://www.militaryonesource.mil/for-spouses.

Military Culture

I have spent a good portion of my own career consulting to organizations on culture change. A healthy, strong culture is critical to an organization's long-term success, but making changes to culture is a tricky business because it is so intangible. I often use a fishbowl metaphor when describing organizational culture. Culture is the water in the bowl that the fish swims in and needs to survive, but he may not even be aware of its presence. Like water, culture slips through our grasp when we try to hold it. Yet, it moves and changes in fluid and natural ways and sustains the life of an organization just as water sustains a fish in his bowl. In any organization, including the military, culture is the overall set of unspoken rules and norms, much like the laws of nature that keep the fish swimming in circles around his bowl. Culture guides the way we do things and the way we don't do things, and newcomers learn the rules through trial and error, sometimes by swimming blindly into the glass of the fishbowl they didn't even know was there. That's how we learn what kinds of behavior are safe and acceptable within a given culture.

The military culture exudes many positive norms, such as patriotism and service, courage and dedication. Our culture values community and family, and we take pride in supporting each other. We value integrity and leadership, and the military is often seen as a role model for these characteristics.

At the same time, however, our military community continues to cling to some outdated norms that no longer represent reality and have negative implications for military spouses. Although the majority of military spouses are either employed or wish to be employed,[22] military culture is still built on an often false assumption that there is a stay-at-home spouse. Aspects of this

[22] As discussed in Chapter 1, about half of all spouses work (Defense Manpower Data Center, 2015), and 60% of those who are not currently employed say they would prefer to be working (Blue Star Families, 2016a).

assumption can be seen in a variety of cultural clues. Spouses' clubs, for example, often continue to hold daytime activities when many are at work; military units still expect spouses to volunteer their time in support of military initiatives. Perhaps most telling, however, is what is said and not said in our informal settings. As Roberta notes in her story, there is still a norm in military social circles that spouses are defined largely by their military member's job, not their own. It is common to talk about what military members do, but far less common to talk about what spouses do. Considering the fact that most of us have a career of some type, this reflects a distinct disconnect between tradition and reality. In many ways, our military is a cutting-edge organization, but in this respect, we seem to be reluctant to let go of an outdated norm that no longer reflects who we actually are.

When I talk about changing military culture with respect to spouse employment, some people take offense. They sometimes think I'm criticizing spouses who choose not to work, and that is definitely not the case. I have chosen to stay home at different points in my family life, and am grateful that I had the freedom not to work at those times. I don't want anyone to lose that freedom. I simply want to see a culture that promotes the same freedom for those spouses who desperately want to work and find it difficult to do so. In an ideal world, both options should be equally attainable and acceptable.

Gender Inequality

I believe the culture conflict I just described is tightly linked to the demographics of the military community. Because the military has traditionally been a predominately male institution, the vast majority of military spouses are female. As such, this gender breakdown exacerbates the spouse employment dynamic in several ways. First, it is still much more acceptable for a woman *not* to work than a man. I suspect if hundreds of thousands of male spouses were unemployed and underemployed, military spouse

194

employment would be considered a national crisis. Instead, female spouses are told it's okay to stay home or that it may even be healthier for their families to do so. Family obligations and childcare issues have become an insurmountable barrier to many spouses who wish to work, but feel they have no real choice beyond the role of full-time homemaker.

Second, as long as spouse employment remains an issue, it will be harder to attract and retain women in the military as service members. Based on traditional gender norms, male spouses have typically been less amenable to becoming the "trailing" spouse who follows a female military member from assignment to assignment, sacrificing his career plans as a result (Cooke & Speirs, 2005). In fact, Cooke and Speirs found in their study of military families that gender was the primary driver of migration decisions, not economics, and that potential earnings of the female spouse were often underestimated by the male partner. In other words, family career decisions most often favor the man's career, regardless of the economic impact. If this is still the case, women may be less likely to get into the military or stay in the military if they have a partner worried about *his* career. This now becomes a vicious cycle. To have more egalitarian gender roles, we need more women in the military ranks, but attracting and retaining them depends on having a lifestyle that allows both male and female spouses to thrive in their careers.

So, what can be done about this? In some ways, this is another aspect of culture change; and I also believe this is an area for further study. Just as I have gathered stories about the experiences of female military spouses, there is a need to conduct a similar inquiry into the lives of female military service members and their male military spouses. How are their lives different? What allows them to thrive that may help us promote a more egalitarian culture going forward?

Michelle Still Mehta

Personnel Assignment System

Lastly, I believe there is one policy area ripe for exploration. There is plenty of evidence that the current PCS system is devastating for military spouse careers, yet most of the efforts made are to accommodate this system rather than change it. Furthermore, this traditional method of reassignment is costly and inefficient for the military. The Government Accountability Office (GAO) has found that moving service members and their families costs DoD $4.3 billion per year, an expense that has risen by 14% in 14 years, despite the fact that the number of overall PCS moves has dropped (Olson, 2015). It is time for DoD to take a comprehensive look at the assignment system and find a new solution that will better serve the military mission and support dual-career families.

Throughout this book, I have discussed the ways in which frequent relocation negatively impacts spouse employment. One reason the impact is so severe is that these relocation decisions are largely unpredictable and uncontrolled by the service member and his or her family. I believe there would be significant improvements in spouse employment and overall satisfaction with military life if service members had more control over their assignments, with more information about available jobs and greater input into assignment preferences.

Replacing the traditional top-down bureaucratic assignment system with a more transparent and organic process is exactly what economist and Air Force veteran Tim Kane (2012) has called for in his critique of the military's personnel system. In essence, he argues that the current system serves no one. In its current form, military members often have little input into their assignment process, and commanders and personnel officers do not have enough information to make good assignment choices. As a result, poor decisions are made that impact the quality of life for military members and their families while also being suboptimal for the military as an organization.

Kane offers a proposal for the future that I find promising. A reformed assignment system should be transparent, much like a traditional hiring process, in that service members should be able to search a database of jobs becoming available with relevant job descriptions and desired qualifications. Service members should be able to bid on jobs they are qualified for and submit all the relevant information commanders and staff need to select the right person. At the end of the process, commanders would still have the ability to make assignment decisions, but service members would have much more information about their options and greater opportunity to communicate their preferences, while taking into account the needs and desires of their family members.

Let me share a modified example from Kane's book to illustrate how this could play out. Imagine a current-day scenario where one service member receives an assignment that he did not request nor desire, only to find out that a colleague desperately wanted that assignment because his wife had a job opportunity there. In this scenario, both needs could have potentially been met if there had been a better process. If the assignment opportunities were made transparent to them, service member and spouse could have searched for assignments that met both of their employment needs and then made their preferences known. In the end, a better decision could have been made to benefit everyone, including the military itself.

In recent years, DoD has recognized that it is facing a looming talent crisis, with shortages in pilot career fields already taking their toll (Losey, 2018). As many as 1 in 4 fighter pilot billets have consistently gone unfilled, a trend exacerbated by the lure of higher salaries and a better quality of life offered by commercial airlines. Under President Obama's administration, Defense Secretary Ash Carter's Force of the Future initiative launched a new focus on attracting and retaining service members, looking for ways to create more flexible career paths for military members traditionally constrained by an "up or out" system (Pellerin, 2016). Policymakers and subject matter experts have made the need for personnel reform clear, noting that DoD's ability to attract and retain talent depends heavily on its ability to meet the needs of dual-career families (Bipartisan Policy Center, 2016). I believe that changing the assignment system needs to be a key aspect of personnel reform.

A more transparent assignment process with greater service member input would benefit both military families and the military itself. Military spouses would have greater insight into their service members' options, and would be able to request assignments that meet their own employment needs. In turn, having more control over assignments would lead to greater satisfaction with military life, and enhance long-term retention of talent.

The good news is that the Air Force has begun experimenting with just such a system for officer assignments through the implementation of its Talent Marketplace (Bailey, 2018). With the introduction of this technology platform, officers in some career fields are able to search for assignments, advertise their availability, and submit their preferences to their assignment officers. This program is certainly a positive step forward that I hope can be expanded to all ranks and career fields, and eventually replicated in other branches of service.

What You Can Do

It is almost always easier to identify problems than it is solutions, especially for an issue as complex as military spouse employment. I don't want to suggest that there is one easy solution to the current situation faced by military spouses, but I do believe there are significant actions we can take both as individuals and as a community. It begins by using our voices to raise awareness with those who may not understand our experiences, and hopefully changing our culture in the process.

If we believe military culture needs to change in the ways I described earlier, what influence do we have in creating such change? Again, I believe our power is in our voices and our stories. The first step toward meaningful change is to simply start talking openly about our challenges. As a practitioner, I have long subscribed to the enactment theory of change that says the way to make large-scale change is to talk differently about the thing you are trying to change (Weick, 1995). When members of an organization or a community start saying things that haven't been said before, or sharing them in a different way, the rules of the road begin to change and cultural shifts can happen quite dramatically.

Many of us have witnessed a very public example of this kind of quantum culture shift in the recent #MeToo movement. By courageously sharing their stories, thousands of women have raised awareness overnight about the pervasiveness of sexual assault. They have not fixed the problem overnight, but they have changed the dialogue about it significantly. Through this movement, our collective society has begun to understand a reality that most women have understood for a long time – that inappropriate sexual behavior is commonplace but rarely spoken about.

I believe the same potential for culture change exists for spouse employment if we, as military spouses, honestly share our stories of sacrifice that we would otherwise bear in silence. I am not suggesting that our situation is akin to the experience of sexual assault or harassment. However, just as in the #MeToo movement, we have the power to change the culture by honestly sharing our pain and disappointment, making the world aware of the suffering that can and should be remedied.

I realize this is no small task, especially for those of us who have been part of a military culture that values being polite, following the rules, and not calling attention to ourselves. Like Roberta, most of us have learned the military cultural norm that we talk about our spouses' careers at social events, but rarely our own. We have learned to compartmentalize and keep a certain part of ourselves for military circles, perhaps leaving the professional side for the office or civilian friends.

You can begin by sharing your story in small ways. If you've been holding back your opinion or experience, start sharing it when the opportunity arises. This doesn't have to be a campaign, rather a shift in mindset to bring the significance of military spouse employment out into the open. Utilize whatever vehicle works for you – social media, one-on-one conversations, or social groups you belong to. Tell your legislators that this issue matters to you. If you receive surveys from DoD or private organizations, take the time to provide your input.[23]

You could also start a support group among your friends, within your neighborhood, in your unit, or in an online community. I've used group coaching programs to promote discussion on this topic, and this is something you could do yourself. All you need is a group of military spouses willing to get together and discuss the stories and reflection questions in this book. Use it to bring your own employment challenges to the table and gain the wisdom of your peers who have also been there. Get together over coffee and start talking. You might be surprised where the conversation leads or what ideas you can generate by supporting each other.

Closing Thoughts

Perhaps the greatest obstacle to seriously addressing the spouse employment issue is that of mindset. I'm reminded of Albert Einstein's famous quote: "We cannot solve our problems by using the same kind of thinking we used when we created them."[24]

---

[23] The annual Blue Star Families Military Family Lifestyle Survey is conducted every spring, and can be found at https://bluestarfam.org/survey. This survey is open to service members, veterans, and military family members.
[24] https://www.brainyquote.com/quotes/albert_einstein_385842

Change is only possible if our leaders are open to new ways of doing things, and sometimes this is not the case.

A few years ago, I was invited to a spouse symposium and participated in a discussion with senior military leaders. When I asked one of them what he thought about changing the assignment system to reduce the impact of frequent relocation on spouse employment, his response was something like, "The PCS system will never change; but don't worry, there are plenty of resources now to help you with your career."

I was chagrined that such a senior leader was convinced there was no reason to change the assignment system, and that he was satisfied that spouse employment had been adequately handled. I believe most leaders now recognize that the spouse employment problem has *not* yet been fixed, but I'm convinced that it will remain a problem until DoD leadership is willing to consider making significant personnel reforms.

Although change is slow in a large bureaucratic institution like the military, I am hopeful that the day will come when spouse employment will significantly improve. We have come a long way in raising awareness on this topic during my tenure as a spouse, and I believe the incoming generation of spouses will continue to demand change. If my children choose military service, I hope they will find a culture that enables their spouses to choose a rewarding career right along with them. The possibilities are endless if we only dare to dream and use our voices to make those dreams a reality.

References

Bailey, K. (2018, April 19). *AFPC adopting innovative officer assignment system IT platform.* Retrieved from https://www.af.mil/News/Article-Display/Article/1498336/afpc-adopting-innovative-officer-assignment-system-it-platform/

Bipartisan Policy Center (2016). *Losing our edge: Pentagon personnel reform and the dangers of inaction.* https://bipartisanpolicy.org/events/pentagon-personnel-reform/

Blue Star Families (2016a). *Military family lifestyle survey: Comprehensive report.* https://bluestarfam.org/survey

Blue Star Families (2016b). *Social cost analysis of the unemployment and underemployment of military spouses.* https://bluestarfam.org/wp-content/uploads/2016/05/Social-Cost-Analysis-of-the-Unemployment-and-Underemployment-of-Military-Spouses_Final_4-5-1.pdf

Blue Star Families (2017). *Military family lifestyle survey: Comprehensive report.* https://bluestarfam.org/survey

Booth, B. (2003). Contextual effects of military presence on women's earnings. *Armed Forces & Society, 30*(1), 25-52. doi:10.1177/0095327X0303000102

Bureau of Labor Statistics (2015). *Unemployment rates by age, sex, and marital status, seasonally adjusted.* https://www.bls.gov/web/empsit/cpsee_e08.htm

Castaneda, L. W., & Harrell, M. C. (2008). Military spouse employment: A grounded theory approach to experiences and perceptions. *Armed Forces & Society, 34*(3), 389-412. doi:10.1177/0095327X07307194

Cooke, T. J., & Speirs, K. (2005). Migration and employment among the civilian spouses of military personnel. *Social Science Quarterly, 86*(2), 343-355. doi:10.1111/j.00384941.2005.00306

Defense Manpower Data Center (2015). *2015 survey of active duty spouses: Tabulations of responses* (No. 2008-028). Arlington, VA: Author.

Department of Defense (2015). *2015 demographics: Profile of the military community.* Office of the Deputy Assistant Secretary of Defense for Military Community and Family Policy.

Department of Defense (2016). *2016 demographics: Profile of the military community.* Office of the Deputy Assistant Secretary of Defense for Military Community and Family Policy.

Hisnanick, J. J., & Little, R. D. (2015). Honey I love you, but... Investigating the causes of the earnings penalty of being a tied-migrant military spouse. *Armed Forces & Society, 41*(3), 413-439. doi:10.1177/0095327X13512620

Hochschild, A. R. (2012). *The second shift: Working families and the revolution at home* (Rev. ed.). New York, NY: Penguin.

Jervis, S. (2011). *Relocation, gender, and emotion: A psycho-social perspective on the experiences of military wives.* London, England: Karnac Books.

Kane, T. (2012). *Bleeding talent: How the U.S. military mismanages great leaders and why it's time for a revolution.* New York, NY: Palgrave.

Lim, N., Golinelli, D., & Cho, M. (2007). *"Working around the military" revisited: Spouse employment in the 2000 census data.* Santa Monica, CA: RAND Corporation.

Little, R. D., & Hisnanick, J. J. (2007). The earnings of tied-migrant military husbands. *Armed Forces & Society, 33*(4), 547-570. doi:10.1177/0095327X06298732

Losey, S. (2018, April 11). The military's stunning fighter pilot shortage: One in four billets is empty. *Military Times.* https://www.militarytimes.com

Maury, R., & Stone, B. (2014). *Military spouse employment report.* Syracuse, NY: Institute for Veterans and Military Families.

Mehta, M. S. (2012). *Work, self, and military life: The experiences of U.S. Air Force wives* (Doctoral dissertation). Fielding Graduate University, Santa Barbara, CA. Retrieved from ProQuest Dissertations and Theses database. (UMI No. 3502622)

Olson, W. (2015, September 10). GAO report says PCS costs rising even as number of moves drops. *Stars and Stripes*. https://www.stripes.com

Pellerin, C. (2016, June 9). *Carter unveils next wave of Force of the Future initiatives*. Retrieved from https://dod.defense.gov/News/Article/Article/795625/carter-unveils-next-wave-of-force-of-the-future-initiatives/

Segal, M. W. (1986). The military and the family as greedy institutions. *Armed Forces & Society, 13*(1), 9-38. doi:10.1177/0095327X8601300101

Weick, K. (1995). *Sensemaking in organizations*. Thousand Oaks, CA: Sage.

Acknowledgments

I am indebted to the women in this book who generously shared their stories with me, even when it was difficult for them to do so. Although I only spent a few short hours with each one of them, they have become precious individuals to me. Thank you for letting me, a complete stranger, into your most private thoughts and feelings.

I am grateful to my editor, dear friend, and fellow military spouse, Tracy DeStazio, for keeping me on track, listening to my ramblings, and engaging in venting sessions now and then. Most of all, thank you for your amazing attention to detail and valuable input on my drafts. I could not have done this without you.

My friends and colleagues that provided support and feedback along the way are too numerous to mention; however, I must highlight a few key individuals that played a vital role in this project. Margo Okazawa-Rey, my academic mentor and role model, held my hand throughout the research and writing processes, and taught me that the greatest gift of love is to see someone for who they really are. Your compassionate activism is a constant source of inspiration to me. Jane Jorgenson first suggested that I look at my military spouse experience as a possible dissertation topic when I was still grappling with my identity as a military spouse. Thank you for supporting me through the research process and partnering with me on several projects since then. Your guidance has been invaluable. Patti Millar was my friend and coach throughout this project, helping me bring this book to life in so many ways. Thank you for your mindful presence and loving support. Karen Hart generously offered her communications expertise on this project and demystified the process of what happens after the book gets written. Thank you for helping me get this book out into the real world. Finally, I am grateful to all my friends and fellow military spouses who gave me feedback and encouragement throughout all the fits and starts of this project.

Without my family, this book would not exist. I am grateful to my husband, James, who always encourages me to take any path

I choose, and patiently gave me the space to complete this project over the course of far too many years. I would not trade you or our military experience for anything in the world. To my children, Sarah and Andrew, thank you for being you and for reminding me every day what matters most.

Made in the USA
Lexington, KY
06 August 2019